American Character and Foreign Policy

EDITED BY
Michael P. Hamilton

William B. Eerdmans Publishing Company
Grand Rapids, Michigan

Copyright 1986 by Wm. B. Eerdmans Publishing Co.
255 Jefferson Ave. SE, Grand Rapids, Mich. 49503
Printed in the United States of America

Library of Congress Cataloging-in-Publication Data

American character and foreign policy.

    Contents: Formative events from Columbus to World
War I / Marcus Cunliffe, Robert L. Beisner — The modern
age / John L. Gaddis, Charles M. Lichenstein — Religious
influences on United States foreign policy / Robert
N. Bellah, Earl H. Brill — [etc.]
    1. United States—Foreign relations. 2. National
characteristics, American. I. Hamilton, Michael Pollock, 1927-   .
E183.7.A545   1986   327.73   86-11564

ISBN 0-8028-0231-1

Contents

About the Editor

The Reverend Canon Michael P. Hamilton is canon at Washington Cathedral in Washington, D.C., where he is responsible for organizing ecumenical and international conferences relating the Christian faith to new scientific, social, and political events. He has long been involved in the concerns of peace and disarmament and serves on the Episcopal Diocesan Peace Commission. Canon Hamilton has contributed numerous articles to secular and religious journals and is also the editor of several books, which include *To Avoid Catastrophe: a Study in Future Nuclear Weapons Policy* (Eerdmans, 1978) and *A Hospice Handbook: A New Way to Care for the Dying* (Eerdmans, 1980).

Preface

Once upon a time, Americans could afford the luxury of isolationism through the grace of two oceans. Now that has changed. Americans are linked inextricably to other continents, militarily and politically, through trade relations, communications, and new modes of travel. These factors have obliged us to assume international responsibilities. Those responsibilities have been heightened within the last forty years by the forging of a radically new international link. The United States and the USSR are vulnerable to mutual destruction because of intercontinental ballistic missiles. Our national security lies hostage to the goodwill of a nuclear adversary. This is a novel political reality that we, with all the nations of the world, are still trying to accommodate.

Traditionally, the United States guarded its well-being by developing foreign policies that preserved a measure of peace and justice in the world while maintaining our own, and our allies', national security. In this age of superpower confrontation, the United States needs clearsighted policies sensitive to a fair balance between our hopes and the legitimate demands of other nations, while protecting the free world from the expansionist tendencies of communist countries.

We cannot indulge ourselves in delusions either about others or—equally important—about ourselves. Poor diplomatic judgment between the superpowers will lead to crises that carry a far graver risk than the possibility of conventional war ever presented. Has our past equipped our leaders and our public to have a reasonably objective perspective on the world? Have our recent policies reflected such a maturity?

The American involvement in Vietnam and more recently in Lebanon are examples of inadequate preparation and unrealistic hopes. On the other hand, most people agree that United States policy toward Japan and Europe after World War II was enlightened and mutually beneficial. Why is our judgment so uneven?

Part of the reason for this inconsistency lies in the fact that foreign policy issues usually come to our attention only during a crisis. The public as a rule has had little preparation to grasp the historical antecedents of the current crisis or to understand our own national bias in relation to them. International conflicts are complex, and in times of excitement Americans fail to recognize that successful diplomacy depends upon considerable background information about the other nation, accurate knowledge of our military and economic abilities, and a careful assessment of the consequences of intervention.

Another reason for foreign policy inconsistency is that we have inherited from our past a confusing mixture of motivations for our actions. These conflicting motivations are the subject of much of the debate over proposed policies which take place in administrative circles, in the press, and in the public consciousness. Philosophies and emotions ranging from isolationism to interventionism, idealism to cynicism, machismo to compassion, all either consciously or unconsciously affect the formation of United States foreign policy. These powerful, domestic psychological pressures ultimately determine what our voters will or will not support. Hence, an informed public, a public which understands the origins of these conflicting motivations, is an essential basis for enlightened policies.

In the chapters which follow, we will be looking beyond the details of specific crises to focus on those cultural, political, economic, and religious events which formed an identifiable "American character." The authors, representing various disciplines, do not attempt a complete historical review. Rather, they concentrate on identifying those past events that in some way remain an influence on our present thinking. In some areas two authors have been invited to express their opinions, the second in response to the text of the first.

A third reason underlying the inconsistency in the quality of United States foreign policy lies in our reluctance to learn from past mistakes. To be able to reflect on political and military defeats requires a national maturity which is itself dependent upon possessing certain cultural and religious attributes. If we tend, for example, to be perfectionist in our expectations of human nature, we will believe that it is possible for leaders always to be right. Mistakes are then interpreted as being politically treasonable and personally unforgivable. When that attitude is dominant, everyone has to defend everything he or she does because society looks for scapegoats to punish rather than complexities to unravel.

There are, I believe, other more realistic understandings of human nature available to us. For instance, if we believe that humans are a mixture of both good and bad, competency and incompetency, then we can avoid the paranoia that sees all errors as sinister. We can reflect with less anxiety about our past, and our imaginations are freed to learn from it. Without a measure of forgiveness, there can be no growth in national self-understanding. Without such a generosity of spirit, both toward ourselves and our adversaries, small disputes that could be easily resolved can escalate to crisis proportions.

However, let it be noted that the Judeo-Christian understanding of human nature does not imply that sweet reason accompanied by full knowledge will bring peaceful solutions to every dispute. There is an undeniable reality to evil—and the attraction of dominating others is both a personal and a national temptation. Those countries which live by the sword, which put most of their efforts into defending their self-interest by building military strength rather than trying to seek justice through international diplomacy, will probably die by the sword. But it is also true that the dovelike qualities of righteousness, reason, and prayer are no substitute for the necessary, serpentine skill of building alliances and acquiring enough military forces at least to deter an enemy.

I wish to thank Provost Charles A. Perry, whose broad vision of the ministry of Washington Cathedral enabled me to undertake a project such as this book represents. Under his leadership the cathedral continues to bring to prayerful public attention all kinds of issues in God's world which deserve critical analysis from a Christian perspective and from the many other secular sources of God's truth. I am also grateful to Professor Robert Beisner and Alton Frye, who gave me frequent and most helpful advice; my wife Eleanore, who shared her wisdom as we talked through its goals and execution; Nancy Montgomery, communications director at Washington Cathedral, who as text editor made many rough places smooth; and Sharon Glass, who as my program assistant kept the correspondence and administration in good order.

The financing of this venture came in part from cathedral and Episcopal diocesan funding, but also from a cathedral endowment established in the memory of Senator A. S. (Mike) Monroney. This fund was established to support the examination of public policy from a Christian perspective, and I am most grateful to the senator's widow, Mary Ellen Monroney, and friends of that generous-spirited and wise senator who, by their donations, have made possible this book and the two public forums held in conjunction with it.

In spite of all this assistance, I expect I have done things I ought not to have done, and not done some things readers would wish me to have done. I hope nonetheless that this study in national self-understanding is sufficiently stimulating to provoke further exploration of its theme. As I pointed out earlier, this ongoing task may well be necessary for our future survival.

MICHAEL P. HAMILTON

AMERICAN CHARACTER
AND
FOREIGN POLICY

CHAPTER I

Formative Events from Columbus to World War I

Introduction

From the very beginning, the first explorers and early settlers possessed certain attitudes of mind which have formed the American character. America was the symbol of the "exceptional" to its immigrants, and as a continent it combined novel physical attributes with a powerful symbolic force. To some it was a second Eden, to others a land turned over to a God-chosen people who had the moral right to control the destinies of the nations around it.

Professor Marcus Cunliffe illustrates these concepts, and they strike familiar chords in our ears. America, "the nation of nations," "the home of the free," has hesitated hardly at all before imposing its political and economic will wherever its shadow fell. Over this policy of national self-interest, America has repeatedly placed a mantle of moral righteousness. In our beginnings we recognize our present—and speculate whether, for good and for ill, those beginnings also forecast our destiny. Or might we, by understanding ourselves better, fashion a wiser future?

Professor Robert L. Beisner identifies the ambiguities in American foreign policy which we inherited from our early past. If we found our political independence in a spirit of anticolonialism, how can we make sense of our own continental expansion at the expense of the American Indians? If we found our national identity through revolution, why are we so hostile to revolutionary movements such as those we encountered in Mexico, the Soviet Union, China, and so many other nations?

Marcus Cunliffe was educated at Oriel College, Oxford University, and at Yale University where he was a Commonwealth Fellow. He began his teaching career at the University of Manchester, continued at the Univer-

sity of Sussex, and since 1980 has been University Professor at George Washington University. He has written widely in the field of American history and has published ten books. They include The Literature of the United States (Penguin, rev. ed. 1985), George Washington: Man and Monument (New American Library, rev. ed. 1982) and American Presidents and the Presidency (McGraw-Hill, rev. ed. 1976). He is currently working on a book about republicanism in America.

ROBERT L. BEISNER received his M.A. and Ph.D. in history at the University of Chicago. He taught at that same university and also at Colgate, and he is presently chairman of the department of history at American University. He is the author of Twelve Against Empire: The Anti-Imperialists, 1898–1900 (McGraw-Hill, 1968; new edition, University of Chicago Press, 1985), which won the American Historical Association's John Dunning Prize, and From the Old Diplomacy to the New, 1865–1900 (Harlan Davidson, Inc., 1975; second edition scheduled for 1986). He is presently at work on The American Diplomatic Tradition for Oxford University Press.

I A
MARCUS CUNLIFFE

I recognize the apparent absurdity in trying to cover more than four hundred years in one short essay. Ralph Waldo Emerson spoke mockingly of his own lyceum lectures, for which he usually chose large, abstract themes. They seemed, said Emerson, "to vie with the brag of Puck: 'I can put a girdle round about the world in forty minutes.' I take fifty."

But then, Emerson did perceive a value in the very range of the endeavor. We too need to generalize in order to perceive, even at the risk of oversimplification and accordingly of distortion. I have picked out a few conspicuously obvious topics (stopping short of the end-of-century controversies that are the particular field of interest of Professor Beisner), with the notion that we tend to overlook precisely what *is* obvious. I am primarily concerned with broad American *attitudes* and *perceptions*, and then, to a secondary degree, with the problem of whether these have tended to be misperceptions.

CHRISTOPHER COLUMBUS

In such a simplified, dramatized perspective, Christopher Columbus is a highly significant *symbolic* figure. For the United States, he above all symbolizes early American yearnings for national independence. He was the hero of the first attempt at a United States verse epic, Joel Barlow's *Vision of Columbus* (1787; revised as *The Columbiad*, 1807). Barlow portrays Columbus as a visionary patriarch, the "great Observer" enabled to gaze down from the stratosphere upon the struggles of the American Revolution and upon the whole process of colonial and national growth.

The new nation solemnly commemorated the three-hundredth anniversary of Columbus's venture. Baltimore erected a column to the explorer in 1792, and New York City's St. Tammany Club held a parade on Columbus Day, October 12. A century later the historian John Fiske fastened upon Columbus's 1492 voyage and landfall as perhaps the greatest event in the whole of human history. In my youth in England, however, there were more equivocal references. A common motion for school debates followed some such rubric as: "That this House regrets

3

Columbus ever discovered America." It served as a convenient topic on which to hang defenses of the democratic creed on one side of the house, and denunciations of jazz, Hollywood, racism, materialism, Yankeedom, etc., on the other side.

Two aspects of the recurrent emphasis on Christopher Columbus as American symbol are particularly relevant. We should note, first, a persistent, deep-lying assumption of American "exceptionalism." Ever since the movement for independence, the inhabitants of the United States have been regarded, by themselves and by people of other continents, as fundamentally different from the citizens of the Old World. To admirers and patriots the difference embodied a superiority: "exceptionalism" meant "being better than" other people, especially Europeans. To critics, many of whom were Europeans, exceptionalism implied inferiority—"being worse than" societies in the older continents.

This pro-and-con exceptionalism predated the emergence of the independent United States. Eighteenth-century *philosophes* frequently maintained that the flora and fauna, and also the human beings, of the New World in both Northern and Southern hemispheres were "degenerate" in relation to those of the Old World. Buffon, DePauw, and the Abbé Raynal argued at one time or another that New World inferiority was manifested in the absence of songbirds, large docile animals like the elephant and the horse, and of other animals (cows, sheep, dogs) suitable for domestication. The human inhabitants were supposedly inferior (in energy, longevity, culture, etc.) to those of the original three continents (Asia, Africa, Europe). An explanation popular among European intellectuals was climatic. Some form of "miasma," they speculated, a debilitating and even toxic atmosphere, perhaps the product of America's low-lying, insect-haunted swamplands, affected all forms of life. Hugh Honour nicely summarized such reactions in his *The New Golden Land: European Images of America from the Discoveries to the Present Time.*[1] He cites the poet John Keats on

> That monstrous region, whose dull rivers pour,
> Ever from their sordid urns unto the shore. . . .
> There bad flowers have no scent, birds no sweet song,
> And great unerring Nature once seems wrong.

The same idea was echoed by the German poet Nikolaus Lenau, who like Keats's brother had an unhappy experience as a pioneer farmer in the United States. "Buffon was right," said Lenau; "in America men and animals deteriorate. . . . I have not seen here a brave dog, a spirited horse, a man full of passion. Nature is terribly languid." Charles Dickens too, in his travel book *American Notes* and his novel *Martin*

Chuzzlewit, appeared to subscribe to the belief that the New World was in general a bad place with an abominable climate.

Among optimists and boosters, conversely, there was a disposition to visualize the New World as a romantic domain where Indian princesses in feathered and golden apparel moved elegantly amid alligators, bison, llamas, and other exotic and remarkable creatures. The admirers of America pictured it as an earthly paradise, a place deliberately set aside by God for latter-day settlement by his chosen ones, and consigned to his special providence. Not surprisingly, the great majority of Americans have preferred the enthusiastic to the gloomy brand of exceptionalism, although the latter has a habit of cropping up, at points of crisis such as the 1860s and 1930s, as a widespread if temporary loss of nerve. In the main, however, there has been much more talk of the American Dream than of the American Nightmare.

The second point about New World-Old World antitheses is the gradual appropriation of "America" by the United States. Early conceptions of the New World, as Hugh Honour makes clear, related mainly to South America or the Caribbean. Bernini's famous baroque fountain in the Piazza Navona, Rome (1651), represents each of the four known continents by a river (Nile, Ganges, etc.). For "America" he takes the Rio de la Plata.

With further exploration and settlement to the north, above all with the achievement of independence by Britain's thirteen mainland colonies and their subsequent successful nationhood, that nation little by little annexed the older continental symbolism. Barlow's *Columbiad* addresses the new country as "Columbia," which of course was the name taken for the federal district in which the new capital of the United States was to be situated. The United States did not for various reasons adopt "Columbia" as its name, nor seize upon other recommendations, including "Alleghania," a designation favored by Washington Irving and Edgar Allan Poe. In the outcome, the "United States of America," originally a plural description rather than a name, remained grandly unspecific. Shortened to "America," it seemed to some neighboring nations to claim the part for the whole, to assert that the United States had some divine right to represent, or even dictate to, the entire hemisphere. Some years ago in Canada I saw a poster, put out not by a radical group but by a Canadian chamber of commerce. The poster bore a picture of a bald eagle, and the caption: "It's Un-American to be Canadian."

The United States thus took upon itself almost the whole mass of historic conceptions of the New World, honorific *and* pejorative. On the whole, I think, Americans accepted this big brother role without any serious misgivings, as a development in the natural order of things. It was implicit in the Monroe Doctrine (1823)—President Monroe's idea that the United States was entitled to speak and if necessary act for the rest of America, North and South, vis-à-vis nonhemispheric nations. Monroe's conception, formulated in conjunction with his secretary of state John Quincy Adams, was of a hemisphere set apart by providence and geography to be a domain of independent republics, free from foreign influence. Theirs was of course a unilateral declaration, not a treaty or convention agreed upon with other nations.

Up to about the time of the Monroe Doctrine, it is true, the United States was in theory prepared to engage in multilateral, pan-American activities: the "good-neighbor policy" of Franklin D. Roosevelt's term. After the 1820s, however, enthusiasm for American involvement rapidly dwindled. The United States did not participate in the 1826 hemispheric convention held in Panama at the behest of the Hispanic-American Liberator Simón Bolívar. Thereafter, the formerly Spanish and the formerly British colonies tended to draw apart from the other.

In theory, the United States accepted the notion of a unique hemispheric destiny, freed from the shackles of colonialism. The notion was, though, perplexing for the other American nations. If American rhetoric were to be taken seriously, old monarchical empires were bound to yield to new republics. Yet President Andrew Jackson appeared in the 1830s to support British claims to the Falkland Islands over those of Argentina. Brazil remained part of an empire linked to Portugal. Canada, despite prophecies of impending annexation by the United States, remained under the British crown. The theory that monarchies were "un-American," while reiterated by American spokesmen of the 1860s during the brief Mexican interlude of the Emperor Maximilian, was undercut by the spirit of "Manifest Destiny" expansionism. According to this new expression of "Yanqui" pride, the Northern, "Anglo-Saxon" peoples were the natural masters of the backward "Mediterranean" races. Joel R. Poinsett, the first United States minister to Mexico, reported home in 1829 that it would be an error to compare Mexicans "with the free and civilized nations" of the modern world. Benighted Mexico was far behind the mother country Spain, itself "notoriously very inferior in moral improvement to all other Nations."[2]

The annexation of Texas and the Mexican War of the 1840s convinced even pro-Americans in the Southern hemisphere that the United States was aggressive and xenophobic. Searching for symbols by which to differentiate their own *Americanidad* or "Americanity" from the *Americanismo* of the North, cultural nationalists such as the Chilean Francisco Bilbao (1823–1865), the Cuban José Marti (1853–1895), the Nicaraguan Rubén Darío (1867–1916), and the Peruvian José Santos Chocano (1875–1934) began to emphasize the ancient Indian heritage, the "Mediterranean" features of Christopher Columbus, and a supposedly romantic, nonmaterialistic spirit blessedly unlike that of the "Hercules-and-Mammon" arrogance of the North. According to the Uruguayan writer José Enrique Rodó (*Ariel*, 1900), the brutish figure Caliban embodied the soulless America of Theodore Roosevelt. It was futile, said Rodó, to try to convince North Americans of the genius of the ancient Mediterranean civilizations, "a work still being carried on and in whose traditions and teachings we South Americans live." How could they explain that such a history "makes a sum which cannot be equalled by any equation of [George] Washington plus Edison"?[3]

The so-called Roosevelt Corollary to the Monroe Doctrine, enunciated in Theodore Roosevelt's annual messages of December 1904 and 1905, indicated still further the gulf between the United States and the Hispanic republics:

> Chronic wrongdoing, or an impotence which results in a general loosening of the ties of civilized society, may in America, as elsewhere, ultimately require intervention by some civilized nation, and in the Western Hemisphere the adherence of the United States to the Monroe Doctrine may force the United States, however reluctantly, in flagrant cases of such wrongdoing or impotence, to the exercise of an international police power.

No doubt there was an American case for some interventions, including a tough line with Britain over Venezuela in 1895. Some of the Latin American nations *were* corrupt and unstable. Nevertheless, American attitudes produced understandable resentment. They struck Hispanic critics as condescending at best, and at worst as hypocritical and no less imperialistic than the military and financial adventurism of the European powers. "Policing," a benevolent activity to those who undertake it, may strike the policed as high-handed coercion. This legacy of mutual disdain and distrust has not been seen in perspective by the average citizen of the United States, in the nineteenth or the twentieth century.

AMERICA AND EUROPE

The "exceptionalism" of the United States gave its citizens an invigorating sense of endeavor and fulfillment. The belief that the new nation was already superior to all others and destined to surpass and supplant those of the Old World acted as a powerful encouragement not merely for native-born Americans but for millions of immigrants. Nationalism was a strong cement throughout the nineteenth-century world. Nowhere was it more fervently and idealistically cherished than in the United States. The inclusiveness of the American claim to be "a nation of nations," an asylum of liberty for the oppressed and a place of opportunity for the world's poor, were visions that formed an essential, and often ennobling, part of the national American self-image.

But nationalism has less likeable aspects. Viewed comparatively as a historical phenomenon, it reveals itself as frequently jingoistic or xenophobic. In his pamphlet *Nationalism: Its Nature and Interpreters* (1976) the historian Boyd C. Shafer notes as one characteristic "a shared disregard for or hostility to other, though not necessarily all, nations."[4] The United States is by no means the only society to have shown disregard and hostility to other peoples. Nevertheless, patriotic pride has often prompted Americans to condemn Old World régimes as backward, undemocratic, immoral, decadent, ultraconservative, and ultraradical, and to assume that converse European criticisms of the United States are "anti-American"—in other words, the product of ignorance and prejudice. In the period 1830 to 1860, for example, Americans from free as well as slave states tended to maintain that British abolitionists had no business to deplore the existence of chattel slavery in North America when their own workers were treated as "white" or "wage slaves." American denunciations of European institutions were delivered with the utmost candor, and with seemingly little concern that such summary verdicts might be resented or repudiated as "spread-eagle" chauvinism.

"Holier-than-thouness" was widespread in nineteenth-century American comments upon foreign countries and foreign policy. We can cull seemingly boastful, antiforeign utterances from even the most thoughtful American men of letters, such as Emerson, Hawthorne, and Melville. Cruder manifestos of the "my country, right or wrong" variety were rife. These generalizations need some qualification. Large numbers of Americans did travel in Europe; Thoreau, Whitman, and Emily Dickinson are almost the only important authors of the century not to visit the Old World. Mark Twain made no less than thirty-one transatlantic crossings. Many Americans retained at least intermittent ties of sentiment with their European origins. By and large, however, the tone of American government and public opinion, as measured by official pronouncements, newspaper editorials, and political cartoons, seems in retrospect complacent and moralistic.

That tone changed somewhat during the course of the nineteenth century. Americans became increasingly less prone to champion European revolutionary upheavals like those of 1848. If monarchs and aristocrats and restrictive trade practices were the *bêtes noires* of earlier American rhetoric, by the 1890s the United States appeared to be more worried by such "foreign" imports as socialism and anarchism. But basic assumptions persisted; the broad frame of exceptionalism seemed to govern discussion. The United States was God's country. Others, whether old or new, monarchical or republican, were inferior. American ideological isolation rested, perhaps, upon a feeling that American democracy could only work within the United States. Other nations, like Britain or Germany, were not yet ready for democracy on the American pattern. Others again, notably in Latin America, perhaps never would be "civilized" enough to introduce the North American model of free enterprise democratic republicanism.

My preceding paragraphs are sprinkled with "seems," "appears," and "perhaps," words intended to suggest that obvious predispositions do not tell the whole story. There is a greater variety in American attitudes than can be rendered by means of crude generalizations about "isolationism" or "expansionism." Thus, one might usefully consider the element of *combined contradiction* in American behavior toward the outside world. The United States, that is, has been *both* isolationist *and* expansionist, sometimes by turns but sometimes simultaneously. "No entangling alliances," the policy of Washington and Jefferson, did not preclude the Louisiana Purchase or Jefferson's miniwar against the piratical principalities of North Africa. The Monroe Doctrine was in part isolationist, yet also expansionist with regard to the role of the United States in the Western Hemisphere.

The United States was, for instance, a trading nation from the start—indeed, the country owned maritime traditions dating from the first English settlements. Tobacco, cotton, and wheat were increasingly cultivated as export staples, aimed at world markets. The active American farmer was as interested in the conditions of international trade as were the merchants and crews of the seaboard towns. The grain belt of the Middle West was, according to the historian William Appleman Williams, keenly in favor of overseas expansion after 1890, even at the risk of war with, say, Great Britain or Spain. Patriotic rhetoric liked to dwell upon images of the American farmer as a "virtuous husbandman," naive and unspoiled. In truth he formed part of a complex system of world trade with whose cycles he kept closely in touch.

Cultural no less than economic involvements with the rest of the world, especially with Western Europe, are attested by the amount of space devoted to foreign news in United States newspapers and periodicals. Movements of shipping, stock prices, shifts in political persuasion, new books and music, and fashions in dress and interior design were keenly watched, together with sheer gossip over births, marriages, deaths, and scandals among the European upper crust. Previous generations of Americans, one begins to suspect, outshone their late twentieth-century descendants in mastery of foreign languages. American diplomacy was conducted on a more modest scale than that of European major powers. Not until the 1890s did the United States upgrade senior

posts from minister to ambassador. American diplomats were instructed to avoid court costume on ceremonial occasions, presenting themselves instead in plain black clothes that (we are told) caused them to be
mistaken for servants. Nevertheless, a high proportion of nineteenth-
century American diplomats and consuls were men of letters—
cosmopolitan figures like Washington Irving, John L. Motley, Charles
Francis Adams, George Bancroft, and James Russell Lowell, who must
have helped to offset European "Yankee Doodle" stereotypes. In other
words, we must beware of supposing that all Americans invariably acted
prior to 1900 as if they believed themselves fundamentally different
from and superior to Europe.

AMERICAN ATTITUDES TO WAR

Alexis de Tocqueville (*Democracy in America*, 1835, 1840) contended
that democracies such as the United States, while not inherently war-
like, waged war when once committed with an all-out vehemence that
left no room for negotiated, compromise solutions. The strategy of
"Unconditional Surrender" Ulysses S. Grant in the Civil War of 1861 to
1865 is often cited in support of this view, together with instances of
supposed American inflexibility in the world conflicts of the twentieth
century. The theory is quite often echoed in current discussion, sometimes with reference to the supposedly "limited" or moderate campaigns of old-style dynastic warfare, as against the bloodthirstiness of
"total" war.

This quite widely held assertion, another example of "exceptionalism," presumes that Americans have fought wars more stren-
uously than Europeans: that is, more ideologically, treating them as
crusades and armageddons instead of calculated, Clausewitzian applications of force ("diplomacy carried on by other means"). The theory
may have some validity in relation to the twentieth century. But as a
generalization about historic formative behavior patterns it fails to hold.
In previous conflicts, surely, the characteristic American expectation
was of campaigns resolved quickly, inexpensively, victoriously, and of
course without permanent allies or consequential alliances. This expectation was borne out, at least in popular interpretation, by the nation's
foreign wars (the War of 1812; the Mexican War of 1846; the Spanish-
American War of 1898) and in most of the fighting with American Indians. None of the foreign wars of the nineteenth century was fanatically
ideological, at least in comparison with, say, the European religious
wars of the sixteenth and seventeenth centuries. Nor did the United
States refuse to consider negotiation or mediation, except in the special
circumstance of the struggle for the Union in the 1860s. Peace discus-

sions were a prominent feature of the War of Independence, again in the 1812 War, and again with Mexico. Some American historians believe the 1812, 1846, and 1898 wars were unnecessary, or that American rhetoric in those crises may have been disingenuous. They have noted opposition to these contests by political or peace-minded groups. But they have not attempted to portray such wars as single-minded *jihads*.

If any long-term lesson can be extracted, it is that wars have rarely been welcomed by the entire American population, and never when their decisiveness is in doubt or their duration prolonged. The expectation, to repeat, has been of swift success followed by an equally swift return to normal peacetime conditions.

Indeed, for a foreign observer such as myself, much in the evolution of American foreign policy resembles that of Great Britain. Both traditionally blended isolationism ("splendid isolation" is the British term) with an energetic quest for markets and influence overseas. Both were expansionist, the British reaching out beyond their island base, the Americans extending their domain (like nineteenth-century Russia) within the continental land mass. Both prided themselves on altruistic moral standards allegedly higher than those of other nations—this to the cynical amusement or exasperation ("perfidious Albion," "Uncle Sham") of those others. Both nations tended in the past to indulge in "vicarious radicalism": namely, a proclaimed concern for the rights of oppressed groups and encouragement to the downtrodden to rise up in revolt, far in excess of any American (or British) capacity or wish to take meaningful action. The American visit of the Hungarian patriot Louis Kossuth after the failure of the 1848 revolutions is a good illustration. American oratory about undying attachment to the cause of freedom prompted him to dream of actual armed intervention by the United States. He alienated American sympathizers by pressing too hard, for instance by telling them that George Washington's isolationist doctrine was outmoded. Soon he was being advised to go back from whence he came. In the military sphere, both Britain and the United States relied for defense upon seas and oceans, tried to cut peacetime military and naval expenditure, and preferred voluntary enlistment to conscription.

AMERICAN EXCEPTIONALISM

This does not mean that American exceptionalist views have been historically insignificant. Notions of a special destiny, mission, or fate have animated much American discourse, religious, political, and patriotic. Such suppositions can be traced in the history of every nationalism, Britain in particular ("God," said John Milton of his own country, "hath not dealt so with any other nation"). But Americans' *belief* in the uniqueness of their New World circumstances, even if somewhat exaggerated, is a central historical datum. Even cosmopolitan Americans, even those highly critical of aspects of their land's foreign policy, have tended under provocation to wave the Stars and Stripes as emphatically as those compatriots whom Kossuth once irritated. Nathaniel Hawthorne wrote of England as *Our Old Home* (1863), but his account had a Yankee tartness not evident from its cozy title.

American exceptionalism, in other words, rests upon an aggregate of subjective and objective factors, details of which can be paralleled elsewhere, but which adds up to a "different" total from that of Britain, Hispanic America, or anywhere else. Racial attitudes in the United States, for example, resemble those of certain other predominantly white nations and have undoubtedly at times shaped American foreign policy. Racism in the United States of a hundred years ago was arguably as manifest as in, say, South Africa and other parts of the British Empire. Yet exceptionalism could in this respect embody tolerance as well as bigotry, with the former gradually triumphing over the latter. The myth of America, that is, as a nation of *all* nations, and as a land of freedom, proved to have more power than the old contrary conception (cherished to a degree even by the Great Emancipator Abraham Lincoln) of North America as a promised land for white Anglo-Saxon Protestants.

One fair conclusion seems to be that the formation of American national character is a complex process, still undergoing modification. The process can be visualized in part as a series of alternations, or perhaps dualisms: a continuing debate between isolation *and* expansion, xenophobia *and* admiration for other cultures (European originally, widening to embrace Asia and Africa), race prejudice *and* multiracialism, moralism *and* expediency. Sometimes the dualisms have managed a mutual accommodation. Sometimes they have collided, leading (as in 1776, 1812, 1846, 1898, 1914, the 1970s) to agonized debate over incompatible impulses.

A second conclusion is that in the long record, public opinion has been prominent in the reckoning—whether for good or ill is a matter for debate. A cynic might insist that public opinion can be manipulated, even in a supposed democracy. How much debate was there before President James K. Polk's administration cajoled Congress into declaring war on Mexico? Still, administrations have ignored public opinion at their peril, and efforts at manipulation have for two centuries been a subject of engrossing interest. An early instance is the propaganda war of the 1770s, in which rebellious Americans like Samuel Adams exercised skill in "working the political engine."

A third and final conclusion is that, historically, exceptionalism has had both desirable and undesirable features.

The bad side has included chauvinistic and sanctimonious truculence: a tendency to overstate American achievements and disparage the contribution of other cultures, or to conceive of world affairs as a battle between virtue (the United States) and evil (x, y, z among other societies). Overblown considerations of national interest in foreign policy have occasionally led the United States to act with impervious belligerence, rationalized as manifest destiny, the white man's burden, or whatever. In response, as we have seen, neighbors to the south have sought to reclaim Christopher Columbus for their own heritage (recalling perhaps that his heroism brought him an ironic recompense—manacled imprisonment in a miserable cell).

The good side of the nonvenerable exceptionalist record of the United States has been its openness to optimism, innovation, and even altruism—the sense celebrated by Emily Dickinson who

> dwelt in Possibility,
> A fairer land than Prose.

The hope for all of us is that in an open debate, on the proposition that Columbus ought never to have discovered America, the doubters will invariably lose, and deserve to lose.

NOTES

1. New York: Pantheon, 1976.
2. Cited in Lewis Hanke, ed., *History of Latin American Civilization: Sources and Interpretations,* vol. 2 (Boston: Little Brown, 1967), pp. 22–26.
3. Ibid., p. 348.
4. Summarized in Boyd C. Shafer, *Nationalism and Internationalism: Belonging in Human Experience* (Malabar, Fla.: R. E. Krieger, 1982), pp. 161–63.

I B
ROBERT L. BEISNER

In examining the long stretch of time from the American Revolution to the age of Woodrow Wilson, I am uneasy at the prospect of isolating a "national character," since the very term embodies so many questionable assumptions, not the least of which is a generally static view of history. The dynamic view of modern historiography would emphasize the evolution of selected characteristics of American diplomacy, including longstanding "policies," some of the values underlying them, and different methods used to carry them out. How some of these characteristics survived into the twentieth century and how others were discarded or modified for new times deserve attention. We should also consider how tensions between policies and values affect our own time—tensions, one could argue, resulting from the American people's view of history as a record of both stability and flux.

A few of the key characteristics of American diplomacy from the end of the Revolution until the autumn decades of the nineteenth century illustrate this dynamic process. Take, for example, the case of isolationism. American isolationism was always selective, intended more as a barrier against entanglement in European affairs than in other regions of the world—especially Asia and Latin America, where the United States never hesitated to act if interests demanded and circumstances permitted. Isolationism so understood represented not only a consciously chosen approach to one facet of international affairs but also an ideologically based fear that the New World experiment could be contaminated and destroyed by the societies and states of the Old World. In addition, isolationism must be understood as a unilateralist approach to the practice of diplomacy—a determination to go it alone even when involvement in faraway lands seemed inescapable.

Americans were seemingly obsessed with neutral rights in the first forty years of national independence, especially the upholding of maritime rights in time of other nations' wars. Officials compiled volumes of commentaries on the doctrine of neutrality in the otherwise sparse files of the State Department. Neutral rights again achieved significance in the months before United States entrance into both of the twentieth-century world wars. During the Civil War, however, Abraham Lincoln and his able Secretary of State William H. Seward had unabashedly executed an about-face, imposing severe restrictions on the right of neutrals who would aid the Confederates.

Felix Gilbert and other historians have identified another characteristic of the early republic's foreign policy—the effort to separate profits from politics. Americans wanted to engage in wide-open trade with all nations while eschewing diplomatic complications and commitments. Although the concept never worked in its idealized form, Americans long tried to have their cake and eat it too, buying, selling, and shipping goods while blithely refusing to acknowledge the inseparability of commerce and political power.

In 1823 the United States pronounced its first foreign policy "doctrine"—James Monroe's—in a series resumed more recently by Presidents Truman, Eisenhower, Nixon, and Carter. Often treating the fifth president's statement more like an *obiter dictum* than a papal bull, American statesmen for many years enforced it with pragmatic selectivity, protesting in vain when unable to do more, winking away violations they thought didn't matter. Nonetheless, the gist of the Monroe Doctrine—that the United States expected to exert a dominant influence in the Western hemisphere—developed into a fundamental goal of United States foreign policy in the nineteenth century.

The historical record has suffered distortion from the common insistence that the United States had a unique proclivity to excess in wars, including an automatic preference that hostilities end with unconditional surrender of the enemy, the defeated bowing helplessly before uncompromising American demands. The first century of this record does, however, reveal characteristic approaches to war. Once diplomacy had failed (sometimes after less than assiduous efforts), the United States would enter hostilities ill prepared, relying heavily on citizen soldiers raised and armed on the spot. A skeleton staff of professionals would then hurl the minuteman force headlong against the foe. Americans favored a strategy of the direct offensive, the better to end the fight in a hurry.

If isolationism was a characteristic ideology, a characteristic product of American foreign policy was expansionism, sometimes achieved with little reference to diplomacy. Texas, Oregon, and California all came into the Union because of the exertion of state power, though the process was aided immensely by the tens of thousands of individual, private choices to head west. From the first days of the republic, Americans were alert for chances to stretch the national boundaries outward. Much of this expansionism, like that of the Roman Empire and the containment policy of Cold War America, sprang from defensive thinking:

"If we don't take (or, in the Cold War, commit ourselves to defend) point A, the fellow just beyond at point B will."

"Now that we've taken point A, we had better take point B, too, or that fellow will always be around to threaten A."

"Well, it sure feels good to have point B to ourselves, but whose outfit is that over the horizon at point C?"

American officials *conducted* foreign policy in characteristic ways, too. For a long time they attempted to carry out a "republican" style of diplomacy—no aristocratic trappings and Old World contrivances for the sons of Columbia. Plain speech and direct dealings, not medal-laden uniforms, extravagant ceremony, and other absurdities of European protocol, would become the New World mode for transacting international business. The republican style, symbolized by Ben Franklin's plain dress and steady gaze, was first reinforced by the general democratization of politics and society, then by a spoils system committed to the premise that any decent citizen could carry on the affairs of state. The ethos of the American republic no more justified elitist airs for international statesmanship than for legislative service.

Officials in Washington usually treated international matters in an ad hoc fashion, waiting passively until something happened that demanded a reaction. Diplomats assigned to legations and consulates in foreign lands rarely had the talents necessary for the posts they occupied. For every John Quincy Adams, the United States seemed to employ ten Rumsey Wings. At the age of twenty-seven, he was appointed by President Grant to Ecuador, which he promptly urged the United States to annex, where he made an attempt on the British ambassador's life, and where he expired from delirium tremens and fever. Like many other American diplomats in the nineteenth century, Wing was a petty politician with poor prospects for work at home in Kentucky. Yet, because Washington seldom anticipated or planned its diplomatic pursuits, these amateur agents found unexpected influence in their hands. The field held the initiative in "making" foreign policy; Washington often found itself relegated to deciding only whether to endorse or cancel what the minister to Mexico or the consul in Kobe had already done.

The Congress that appropriated funds for this so-called "diplomatic service" handled foreign policy just as it would river dredging bills or veterans' pensions—that is, with partisanship and parochial interests uppermost. A State Department that seldom formulated what we might today call "policies" seldom objected.

Apart from defensiveness about over-the-horizon unknowns that provoked the repeated ventures of expansionism, America's diplomacy—both the objectives and the modus operandi—rested on the comforting assumption that the republic was safe from injury, at least after the French Revolution and the Napoleonic wars had played themselves out in 1815. The United States had grown larger and more powerful. Weak neighbors bordered north and south. Europe seemed quiescent, and in any case the only potential enemies strong enough to justify worry were far away, across vast expanses of oceanic defense.

The disappearance of this bedrock assumption of national safety largely accounts for the important changes that occurred in American foreign policy in the period from about 1890 to World War I. Most of these changes had appeared in embryonic form even before Dewey's victory in the Philippines. The defeat of a European fleet thousands of miles from our shores rang the bell announcing the birth of the American Century.

Why these changes occurred is a large subject, but not the subject here. Suffice it to state that internal developments, from massive migration to a shattering depression, combined to challenge the view that America was fated to progress onward and upward forever. This worm of self-doubt suddenly made developments beyond America's boundaries seem more important, as did contemporary international events, including a new burst of European imperialism, the threatened disappearance of foreign markets for American goods, rapid advances in military technology, and the speeding up of communications. Doubts arose about old approaches to foreign policy. An atmosphere of danger —newly perceived—required a novel diplomatic and military response.

As a consequence, Americans overhauled the way they dealt with issues in foreign affairs. A new continuity marked United States diplomacy, with policies on Cuba or China adopted in a Republican administration surviving under its Democratic successor, or persisting despite the transition from one secretary of state to another. Officials became freshly alert to the connections linking different issues. Putting an end to the civil war in Cuba in 1898 was essential for impressing European powers that the United States was serious about supporting its position in China; a strong China policy in turn demanded the annexation of the Philippines; taking over the Philippines meant fastening control over the Hawaiian islands once and for all; having subscribed to such large new tasks in the Pacific and East Asia, policy makers found it imperative to assure secure lines to the area from America's eastern political and financial centers by digging a canal through Central America; and that having been decided on, United States officials could no longer refrain from intervening in the affairs of Caribbean nations to defend the canal's maritime approaches.

Having to deal with such portentous issues also meant the time had come for Washington to seize the reins of policy. Thus, while diplomats sent abroad were upgraded in quality, they were also restricted in freedom, for the diplomatic initiative shifted decisively from the field to the center. Soon a professional foreign service came into being. On a parallel track the military services, especially the navy, revamped armaments as well as strategy to prepare for a more perilous world.

Officials now thought of the United States as a great power, even a world power, with interests spread over the globe—not only in Cuba, Mexico, and Canada, but in Venezuela, China, the Congo, Korea, and elsewhere. And officials formulated "policies" to deal with these new interests. They instructed their diplomats to carry out these policies and reprimanded them if they did not. A dangerous world would require discipline as well as strength.

Given such a transformation, one might think that most of America's old diplomatic traditions and values would be swept aside in a flourish. Some were, but most survived in one form or another, although not always in a comfortable fit with the new times. Certainly the "republican" style of diplomacy faded into the background if it did not disappear altogether. The architecture of American missions improved noticeably; diplomats were finally appointed at the rank of ambassador; and the State Department began seeking recruits in the halls of Harvard and Princeton rather than the political precincts of Chicago and Kentucky. Military patterns changed greatly, too, although a stubbornly stingy Congress would long cramp the style of army and navy reformers.

By 1919 isolationism as a refusal to participate in the affairs of the world was extinct, though it persisted in the continuing opposition to ties of alliance and commitment with other nations. In World War I neutral rights resurfaced as a major issue, but far less in the guise of an ideological absolute than as a specific aspect of the American national interest. The idea of pursuing commerce without politics was replaced by an aggressive diplomacy dedicated to opening doors to American traders. The American sense of mission, the belief that the United States had a special role to perform for all nations, changed from the passive conception of providing an example for others to emulate to the activist belief in a duty to export institutions, principles, and other blessings from America's cornucopia to the benighted abroad.

Other traditions and values were strengthened, reinforced by the new seriousness and activism of American foreign policy. This was true especially of the Monroe Doctrine, now definitely placed in the pantheon of American doctrines. It was also true of expansionism, or imperialism, which entered its generation-long heyday in 1898, especially in the form of Caribbean interventionism.

But two ominous changes also took place among the values underlying American foreign policy. Both warrant extensive analysis but can only be mentioned here.

First, a nation born in the first modern anticolonial revolution, its people self-identified as pioneering anti-imperialists, became imperialists themselves. Hair-splitting about terms cannot efface the imperialism of the Indian wars, the forcible annexations of both contiguous and distant territories, or the interventions and bayonet-backed political tutelage in Cuba, the Dominican Republic, Haiti, Mexico, and Nicaragua. Historians have yet to offer a convincing analysis of how the people and leaders of the United States converted to imperialism without acknowledging what they had done. Though they did mute overt invocations of traditional anti-imperialism, they drew imaginatively from a dictionary of denial in finding the language—protectorates, expansionism, Roosevelt Corollary, hemispheric security, containment—that would provide the tongue and mind a way to evade confessing what still felt like the crime of imperialism. Imperialism by any other name, they persuaded themselves, is *not* imperialism.

Akin to this development was the new conservative reaction to dramas of revolution abroad. Where Americans had once applauded, they now sat silent in the galleries, soon to break out in hisses and catcalls. Thus, the United States not only expelled Spain from Cuba and the Philippines, it put an end to the revolutionary movements in both places. Soon to follow were its ambivalent or even hostile responses to revolutions as disparate in character as those in Mexico and Hungary, China and Russia. Once again, Americans denied what was happening—to themselves. A "violent" or "alien" revolution was not a true revolution, but a sinister disorder contrary to the popular will.

Additional significance in these changes in American foreign policy values lies in their connection to one another, for American imperialism in the past ninety years has commonly been aimed at suppressing or rechanneling the revolutions of other societies.

The United States embarked on the twentieth century with a new outlook on the world. Unlike the sunny assumptions of safety held as recently as the 1880s, this new outlook started from a view of the world as treacherous. Consequently, the United States forged new tools for the practice of foreign policy and national defense. Some old values were tossed aside, a few retained in pristine form, most remodeled for the new age. Both this view of the outer world and the practices it spawned, however altered since, are not radically dissimilar from those in our own times.

From then to now, from the United States-Philippines War to the latest bulletin from Nicaragua, we have lived with policies in which are embedded attitudes flatly contradictory to early American values. We do not openly avow these attitudes—interventionism, imperialism, hostility to revolution—as part of our twentieth-century approach to world politics. As a result, much of our political and intellectual energy for several generations has been directed toward discovering ways to rationalize these contradictions. Americans have been unwilling or unable to reject imperialism or to revive an acceptance of revolution. Nor have they been willing candidly to accept imperialism or endorse openly a commitment to the status quo. Such tension between practice and rhetoric, between acceptance and denial, confuses not only the leaders of other nations but ourselves as well. At what cost, we are still learning.

CHAPTER II

The Modern World: World War I to 1984

Introduction

The rise of America as a world leader is the most important development in our nation's modern history. Was this new role unsought? Did we welcome our newfound ability to influence others? Were we sufficiently sophisticated to understand the nature of this responsibility? Have we ever even come to a clear understanding of our own national self-interest? Professor John L. Gaddis traces the debates which took place within our nation in response to these challenges. In spite of our internal divisions and reluctance to become involved, we participated in two world wars and played decisive roles in their outcome. Our national predisposition to isolationism in principle was fully overcome by these events.

Professor Gaddis also examines the attitude of the United States toward its enemies, particularly Germany and the Soviet Union. Was the United States's antipathy toward them borne of distaste for totalitarian government or for Marxist ideology? Are communist nations necessarily a threat to us, or are some Marxist-inspired national governments also capable of being our allies when our national self-interests overlap? Finally, what balance can be struck on the merits of the use of United States military and economic power in our modern period?

The Honorable Charles M. Lichenstein responds to Professor Gaddis's essay and criticizes it from another perspective. He raises the difficulty of generalizing about the American character as it affects foreign policy. Is each international issue so different that historical generalities should not be drawn? How moral is the content of our foreign policy? Is the desire of the American people to live up to their ideals an overriding influence on policy or is it simply an expedient and additional argument?

John L. Gaddis *is presently the Distinguished Professor of History at Ohio University. He received his M.A. and Ph.D. from the University of Texas. He has been the recipient of a number of awards, grants, and fellowships, and has written widely in the field of American history.* His books include The United States and the Origins of the Cold War, 1941–1947 *(Columbia University Press, 1972),* Russia, the Soviet Union, and the United States: An Interpretive History *(John Wiley, 1978), and* Strategies of Containment: A Critical History of Postwar United States National Security Policy *(Oxford University Press, 1982). His forthcoming books include* The Oxford History of American Foreign Relations *and* George F. Kennan and American Foreign Policy.

Charles M. Lichenstein *received his B.A. and M.A. at Yale University and is presently Senior Fellow in International Relations at The Heritage Foundation in Washington, D.C. His career has been in public affairs and politics, and he served from 1981 to 1984 as alternate United States representative to the United Nations and deputy United States representative to the Security Council. He was a special assistant both to President Nixon and President Ford, and executive assistant to the chairman of the Federal Communications Commission in President Nixon's administration. He has served on the presidential campaign committees for both Richard M. Nixon and Barry Goldwater.*

II A
JOHN L. GADDIS

One of the most remarkable intellectual feats in the history of the modern world took place, it is said, when Sigmund Freud lay down on his couch, or wherever else he did it, to undertake the first and so far the only successful self-examination of one's own subconscious. Self-awareness, after all, is not something that comes easily for individuals: the entire practice of psychoanalysis is based upon the need for an outsider to wrench the truth about ourselves from behind the barricades of deception, evasion, and fantasy with which we surround it.

Great nations behave in much the same way. They tend to resist critical self-evaluation. They throw up barriers behind which they conceal their own inadequacies, contradictions, and anxieties. They lack the capacity to assess objectively—at times even to account for—their own conduct. They require, it sometimes seems, the ministrations of outsiders to force them to come to grips with themselves.

Consider the fact that some of the best books about the English have been written by the French, and vice versa. Consider the irony that an American, Gordon Craig, has compiled what is probably the best guide to the tortured history and psychology of Germany. Consider how little we would know about China and Japan if it had been left to the Chinese and Japanese instead of John Fairbank and Ruth Benedict to interpret them to the rest of the world. And of course Russian studies by definition have relied upon the works of distinguished outsiders, from the days of the Marquis de Custine and the first George Kennan through Bernard Pares, E. H. Carr, Louis Fischer, Merle Fainsod, and of course the second Kennan to the thoughtful contemporary reporting of journalists like Strobe Talbott, Robert Kaiser, Hedrick Smith, David Shipler, and Michael Binyon.

Or consider the best writings about Americans themselves. The classics that come to mind are those by Alexis de Tocqueville or Lord Bryce; the histories one thinks of would certainly include those of Marcus Cunliffe and George Dangerfield; in the realm of popular culture Alistair Cooke has made a career of interpreting, not only the English to the Americans, but the Americans to themselves. Like other nations, we seem to need an outside observer—an analyst, if you will— to make us come to grips with both our achievements and our shortcomings in anything approaching an objective manner. We seem to be no better at doing that ourselves than anyone else is.

And yet, the ultimate intent of psychoanalysis is to provide the patient with at least some capacity for self-diagnosis, with at least some ability to evaluate for one's self the problems one faces and the appropriate solutions for them. Certainly that would be a useful thing for nations to be able to do: after all, to sit around and wait for the next Tocqueville or Bryce might take quite a while. We ought to develop more of a faculty for self-awareness and self-criticism than we have managed to do; we ought not to rely, as much as we do, upon our external analysts for these revelatory insights.

How might we go about it? A necessary first step might be to step back from the periodic outbursts of pride or chagrin with which we regard our conduct in world affairs, and try to get a more detached sense of what we have actually been doing all this time. One useful way to approach this task is to imagine one's self as a history professor in the year 2086, charged with lecturing to a room full of surly, squirming undergraduates on the characteristics of United States foreign policy in the twentieth century. (This exercise proceeds on the pessimistic assumption that undergraduates will still be bored a hundred years from now, but also on the optimistic assumption that there will still be history professors around to bore them.) What would one say under such daunting circumstances?

I, for one, would talk about four particular problems Americans have confronted in attempting to deal with the rest of the world: the problems of power, interests, threats, and consequences. I would try to show that Americans have faced certain recurrent dilemmas in coping with each of these, dilemmas that define, as much as anything else does, a distinctive American "style" in the conduct of foreign affairs. Were I to get that far, I would at that point sit down, on the assumption that that would be quite enough to digest for one day, even a hundred years hence. This essay can be considered a rough first draft of that lecture: it's always a good idea to prepare things well in advance.

First, consider power. I mean by this quite simply the capacity for influence, the ability to make things happen in the world, whether in the military, political, economic, ideological, or cultural realms of human activity. One cannot help but be struck by the extent to which Americans have had that capacity in the twentieth century; no other single nation has come close to rivaling the United States in that respect. Henry Luce's vision of an "American Century" has, in this sense, been confirmed; it is the possession of this power, more than anything else, that distinguishes our experience in this century from the ones that preceded it.

The power we have had came to us partly through inheritance: our forefathers had the good sense to establish themselves and the state they created on land that was not only isolated and uncrowded but also enormously productive in both agricultural and mineral resources. One need only compare the experience of Russia—which also expanded into isolated and uncrowded regions at about the same time—to see how much difference these accidents of climate and geology have made. But environmental circumstances provided only the potential for power; its actual attainment required sweeping away the competition, and this the Europeans obligingly did for us during the first half of the twentieth century.

It makes more and more sense, the further removed in time we are from them, to view the First and Second World Wars as a single European civil war, in which nations that had dominated world politics for the previous several centuries managed to relegate themselves, through their own fratricidal tendencies, to the status of second-class powers. There ensued, as a result, a historic shift of geopolitical influence from the center of Europe to its peripheries, with the United States and the Soviet Union as the ultimate beneficiaries.

But that migration of power away from Europe did not produce new concentrations of power of equal magnitude: for although the Soviet Union would, in time, develop military strength roughly comparable to that of the United States, the passage of time has made clear the extent to which the Russians have failed to compete effectively in the economic, political, cultural, and even the ideological arenas of international relations. The Soviet Union's power, future historians are likely to conclude, rested upon a monodimensional military base; that of the United States has been multidimensional, and that fact—assuming, of course, that we and the Russians can continue to avoid explicit tests of our respective military strengths—is likely to prove decisive.

What is less clear than the fact that Americans have accumulated great power is the extent to which they have consciously sought it. It is too easy to infer, from the reality of power, a coherent strategy for acquiring it. It is too simple to conclude that because a nation has come to dominate much of the rest of the world in a military, economic, and cultural sense, it must have set out to produce this result as a matter of deliberate intent. The gap between what nations seek to do and what they wind up doing is about as wide as it is for individuals; that analogy alone should make us cautious about establishing chains of causation that too rigidly link consequences with the intentions that lie behind them.

For the fact is that Americans have never been very comfortable with power: witness the extremes to which they went to fragment it in their own domestic constitutional arrangements. Nor have they always been certain of their ability to wield power wisely—that is, in ways that would promote their own national interest—in the international sphere. The accumulation of power has been a dominant theme of American diplomacy in the twentieth century, but so too has been a deep and persistent suspicion of it. Let me illustrate what I mean.

The United States had the capacity to become a power of consequence in world affairs long before it actually did. As early as the 1860s, Americans had demonstrated to impressed Europeans what could happen when industrial strength was linked with military purpose. In the decades that followed Europeans watched the progress of economic development and technological innovation in the United States with a keener sense than the Americans themselves of the implications these trends posed for the balance of power in the world. But the actual policies the United States followed in the final decades of the nineteenth century were curiously unassertive for a nation whose population and industrial strength was so rapidly expanding. Certainly no single-minded "drive for world power" animated the thinking of a Grover Cleveland, or a Benjamin Harrison, or even the most hyperactive political figure of his day, James G. Blaine.

Even when we did shift to a more assertive role in the mid-1890s, our hesitancy about wielding power remained. We passed up the opportunity to make Cuba a colony after taking it, by force, from Spain. We did make the Philippines a colony, but we decided almost at once that this had been a mistake and began preparing the Filipinos for independence. We maintained and even strengthened our traditional sphere of economic and strategic influence in Central America and the Caribbean, but made only half-hearted and ineffectual efforts to expand that sphere to East Asia. And despite the fact that a historical accident had brought to the White House in the person of Theodore Roosevelt one of the most sophisticated students of power politics in this century, we played almost no role in European affairs during the years that preceded World War I; the outbreak of that conflict was one of the last great European events with which the United States had absolutely nothing to do.

World War I was, of course, as the historian Daniel Smith has labeled it, "the great departure."[1] The armies we sent to Europe in 1918 had a more decisive impact on the outcome of that struggle than did the much larger forces we sent back to the continent in 1944; certainly no one can deny Woodrow Wilson's dramatic influence on wartime diplomacy or on the drafting of the peace settlement that followed. But even here our distrust of power eventually overcame our appetite for it: we dismantled our military forces almost at once and rejected any role in Wilson's own chosen instrument for managing world politics in the future, the League of Nations. This is not the behavior of a nation with an urge to dominate.

The long-term effects of American participation in World War I came to lie primarily in the economic sphere, in our emergence as Europe's chief creditor and source of investment capital. Historians are only now beginning to grasp the critical role the United States played in the rehabilitation and stabilization of Europe in the 1920s, a role that now seems comparable in importance to our better-known activities in that regard after 1945. But unlike the Marshall Plan of a generation later, our involvement in post-World War I European reconstruction took the form of private initiatives carried out with the tacit support of the government. Given the strength of isolationist sentiment—in itself an indication of how much we distrusted our own power—this was the only way the United States could play any role at all.

Even so, what happened after 1929 makes it clear how important these activities were. Our depression spread to Europe even faster than our earlier prosperity had, thereby demonstrating the extent to which the economies of that part of the world—and indeed those of most of the rest of the world as well—had come to depend upon our own economic health. We had become, by the end of World War I, an economic superpower without wholly realizing it; we had attained that eminence more through the actions of others than by our own choice or will.

It is significant that during the interwar period we made no effort to match our economic influence with any comparable military or political influence. Throughout these years we showed a striking gap between our capacity to shape the world economy and our almost petulant refusal to have anything to do with world politics. It was as if we had rigidly compartmentalized the components of power, and were determined to embrace one and to neglect all the rest. Only the fall of France and the attack on Pearl Harbor overcame this compartmentalization, and even then remnants of isolationism remained. Franklin D. Roosevelt himself, it is true, had no reservations whatever about participation in great power politics, but as an appalled witness to Wilson's failure a quarter of a century earlier, he harbored profound doubts as to whether the American people were prepared to share his view. He showed remarkable caution in not getting ahead of public opinion as the United States moved toward active belligerency between 1939 and 1941, to the point that his friend Winston Churchill despaired of our ever entering the war. Roosevelt's strategy for fighting the war, which critics subsequently would condemn as naive, now appears in fact to have been more sophisticated than anyone suspected at the time: it was to provide to the maximum extent possible the *weapons* with which to defeat Germany and Japan, but to leave to allies—chiefly Russians and Chinese—the expenditure of *manpower* necessary to do this. It would not do, Roosevelt thought, to have the war be too painful an experience for an American public still not fully reconciled to global responsibility.

Roosevelt's strategy worked better in Europe than in the Pacific, where the United States in the end did have to assume the main burden of fighting. But even so, victory came, all things considered, with surprising ease. Our casualties were remarkably light, given the scale and duration of the fighting. We came out of the war with an industrial plant far larger and more advanced than at its beginning; our gross national product had roughly doubled between 1939 and 1945. Our military strength appeared unchallengeable, especially in the light of the development of the atomic bomb. "Of the great men at the top, Roosevelt was the only one who knew what he was doing," the British historian A. J. P. Taylor has commented. "He made the United States the greatest power in the world at virtually no cost."[2]

Whether Americans would pay the price necessary to retain such power, though, was even yet not clear at the end of the war. We did accept, after 1945, political responsibilities we had shunned after 1918, but at the same time we dismantled our military forces almost as thoroughly as we had a quarter of a century earlier. The gap between commitments and capabilities became painfully clear as President Truman launched the effort to contain Soviet expansionism while attempting to hold military spending within limits only slightly above prewar levels. It took not just the appearance of the Soviet Union as a rival in Europe but also the emergence of a perceived threat of communism on a global scale—something that did not happen until the victory of Mao Zedong in China and the onset of the Korean War—to convince the nation of the need for a large peacetime military establishment and for the levels of spending necessary to sustain it.

It was not until mid-century, then, that the United States can be said to have reconciled itself, once and for all, to its status as a superpower, and even then we can hardly be said to have overcome the ambivalences we have felt about the exercise of power itself. Consider, for example, the haste with which we sought to end the occupation of Germany and Japan: even Americans as imperious as Generals Clay and MacArthur did not find the role of overlord a congenial one. Or consider the limitations we imposed upon ourselves in the Korean War and again in Vietnam: no one can claim that we used all the power available to us in those conflicts. Or consider the thoroughness with which we have investigated abuses of power when they have occurred: there can be few parallels in history to the highly public scrutiny given our intelligence agencies in the wake of the Watergate scandal a decade ago.

Or consider, most significantly, our attitude toward the symbol of absolute power itself, the atomic bomb. We had exclusive possession of that weapon for only four years, but Soviet stockpiles and delivery capabilities remained at such primitive levels that the American monopoly for all practical purposes extended well into the 1950s. Nor were opportunities lacking, during this period, for the use of such weapons: their use was seriously contemplated, we now know, in Korea just prior to the armistice agreement in 1953, in Indochina in 1954, and in the Taiwan Strait crisis of 1954–55. We could very well have used them: psychological taboos on military use had not yet had time to develop; Soviet retaliatory capabilities were nonexistent; public opinion would certainly have been prepared to trust Eisenhower's judgment in such a matter. And yet we did not, and the best explanation seems to be that we thought it would look bad to employ such weapons against Asians again so soon after Hiroshima and Nagasaki. In effect, we deterred ourselves, for fear of what the use of such great power might imply about ourselves.

This self-consciousness about the wielding of power distinguishes the American possession of it from that of most other great nations in the past. It is not that we have no appetite for power, although it has been thrust upon us about as often as we have actively sought it. It is not that we consistently try to divest ourselves of power once we have got it, although there have been instances in which we have done just that, whether through design or incompetence. It is simply that we are not wholly comfortable in the role of a great power, that we tend to worry more about it than other great powers have in the past, and that we tend to look, more actively than most other great powers do or have done, for ways to justify the power we have not in terms of power itself, but of some very different end.

That brings up the problem of interests. Nations never wield power entirely in a vacuum. The exercise of power is always informed by some conception of national interest, whether permanent or transitory, rational or irrational, altruistic or self-serving. Another characteristic of American diplomacy in the twentieth century that historians a hundred years from now will probably consider important is the ingenuity with which we have linked the power we possess with both immediate and ultimate interests.

Interests are so basic a phenomenon that they often go unstated. To say that it is in the interest of a nation to survive, to be secure from attack, and to enjoy an international environment reasonably congenial to the prospering of its domestic institutions is only to propound the obvious; all nations share these interests, and all of them attempt to use such power as they command to promote them. Beyond these obvious requirements, though, there can be important differences in the way nations define their interests; certainly the American conception of interests in this century has had some distinctive characteristics about it.

The first and most important of these has been quite simply to keep power balanced. Just as we have historically worried about our own ability to wield power wisely and equitably, so too—and to a greater extent—have we distrusted the abilities of others to do the same thing. We have been sensitive to the danger that others might accumulate power in sufficient quantity to impair our security; where that has happened we have not been hesitant to build up our own power to counterbalance the threat or to form combinations of power with those who shared our perception of the danger at hand.

It would be a profound misreading of American diplomatic history to say that the United States discovered the balance of power only during the twentieth century. The first alliance we ever made, with France in 1778, illustrates with classical clarity the principle of aligning with one power to counteract another, in this case Great Britain, from whom we were seeking independence. Washington's farewell address was hardly an unqualified endorsement of isolationism, but rather an argument for remaining aloof from foreign entanglements until they became necessary to break up potentially hostile concentrations of power. The isolationism that characterized most of nineteenth-century American diplomacy should be understood as a reflection of the fact that no such concentrations of power appeared in Europe between 1815 and 1914. It is significant that when such threats did appear, as they did more frequently in the twentieth century, the United States did manage to put aside isolationism in order to deal with them.

Woodrow Wilson, for example, was thinking in clear balance-of-power terms when he decided that American interests could not tolerate a German victory in World War I: the combination of continental land power with the naval power of a defeated Britain would be too great. Franklin D. Roosevelt took precisely the same view regarding Nazi Germany a quarter century later; similar considerations influenced his decision to get tough with Japan at the same time. And it is clear, now, that American leaders regarded the Soviet Union's expansion into Europe after 1945 as yet another threat to the balance of power; it was this that accounted for yet a third projection of American countervailing strength onto the European continent—although this time without a war—in as many decades. That same concern with potentially hostile aggregations of power shifted to the world at large as the Cold War intensified, so that by the 1950s and 1960s any shift in the global status quo, no matter how minor, could come to seem a threat of vast significance to what were now global American security interests.

But Americans' distrust of power has prevented them from justifying their interest in the balancing of power for what it was: there has always been something too amoral, too cynical, too "European" about that kind of thinking. Instead Americans have sought ways to link their concern with stability to some entirely different concern, whether of a self-interested or a disinterested nature. Quite frequently, in fact, we manage to do both: we seem uniquely adept among the peoples of the world at combining appeals to both base and lofty instincts. We like to convince ourselves that both immediate and ultimate interests are going to be served by what we choose to do.

Take, for example, the concept of multilateralism. The United States has repeatedly called for a reduction of barriers to trade and investment throughout the world on the grounds that the condition of humanity at large would benefit if individual producers were free to concentrate on what they can most efficiently produce. Indeed, Americans have gone farther than that: wars, we have tended to believe, are in large part the product of rivalries that grow out of economic nationalism; if nations could become economically interdependent, we have wanted to believe, war itself might become obsolete. (Never mind that our own tariff policies hardly corresponded to multilateralist principles throughout much of our history, or that the connection between trade, investment, and economic development remains less than clear, or that the historical record suggests little correlation between high levels of economic interchange and the avoidance of war.) And yet, as a generation of revisionist historians have correctly pointed out, multilateralism brings disproportionate benefits to the most efficient producer, and the United States of course has found itself in that position throughout most of the twentieth century. Our disinterested pursuit of multilateralism, therefore, has served our self-interested ambition to expand markets, investment opportunities, and profits. It was an ingenious and potent strategy, although the recent growth of protectionist pressures that has followed the loss of our competitive edge in the world economy says something interesting about the relative importance of the motives that lay behind it.

This peculiar mixture of self-interest and disinterest can be seen as well in the concept of self-determination, one of the most frequently identified American interests in world affairs. It is difficult to argue against the proposition that people throughout the world ought to have the right to choose their own form of government. In fact, Americans have tended to see in the idea of self-determination, as in the idea of multilateralism, a way of abolishing war: if everyone lived under governments of which they approved, what would there be to fight about? But application of the principle of self-determination has coincided suspiciously, over the years, with our own geopolitical interests. Wilson invoked self-determination as a means of breaking up Germany's major ally in World War I, the Austro-Hungarian Empire; he was less keen, though, on applying the same idea to the colonial empires of Great Britain or France. Roosevelt endorsed self-determination, along with Churchill, in the Atlantic Charter; but efforts to apply the principle in Eastern Europe, at a time when we still needed the Soviet Union's cooperation in the war against Germany and Japan, were at best half-hearted. Subsequently, during the Cold War, we insisted regularly upon the need for self-determination within the Soviet Union's sphere of influence, but were a good deal less ardent about applying the principle to anticommunist allies or associates in places like Indochina, Central America, or South Africa. Despite surface appearances, there were no real inconsistencies in these policies: they were all aimed in one way or another at preserving a favorable balance of power in the world. But by refusing to admit that fact, by insisting on the need to cloak the balancing of power behind an idealistic facade, we not only created the appearance of inconsistency, we also gave rise to expectations beyond our capacity to fulfill.

Similar unfulfillable expectations are likely to arise from a more recent appeal to disinterest as a means of justifying self-interest: attempts by both Presidents Carter and Reagan to win support for their efforts to build and deploy additional nuclear weapons by holding out the ultimate goal of abolishing such weapons from the face of the earth. The immediate interest to be served here is clear: there are still enough people around who confuse piety with intentions to make an argument like this worth advancing. But where does the ultimate American interest in this matter lie: in a world free from nuclear weapons, or in a world free from instability, disorder, chaos, and war? If in fact the latter is our interest—and historically that is how we have tended, in our more realistic moments, to conceive of it—then the abolition of nuclear weapons could actually be inconsistent with the goal we seek, since there is reason to think that such weapons have on balance reinforced rather than detracted from international stability during the years of their existence. The four decades of peace we have enjoyed since the end of World War II have been obtained in no small part through the caution in the calculations of statesmen that results from fear: one need only compare the incidence of great power war in the four decades preceeding 1945 to see the point. This is not an argument against arms reduction: one could no doubt achieve the stabilizing effect of nuclear weapons with only a tenth of the number now available in the arsenals on both sides. It is, though, an argument against confusing the instruments of conflict with its causes—two very different things. And it is a warning of the danger of raising expectations beyond what it is realistically possible to achieve.

One sees in all this the risks of not being precise about just what it is we seek. To take the realistic concept of the balance of power and to try to cloak it in idealistic garb—whether of multilateralism or self-determination or nuclear abolition—is not only to confuse our priorities; it is certain as well to produce in the long run the very cynicism and disillusionment we seek to avoid by concealing our realism in the first place.

We are, of course, hardly the only nation in the world that has sought to link immediate interests with ultimate ones. All nations do this to some extent; in this they are not much different from most individuals. But the efforts we have gone to to construct such linkages and the persistence with which we adhere to them do seem to go beyond what most other nations do. What goes even farther—and what surely must constitute a distinctively American characteristic in the conduct of international affairs—is the extent to which we actually believe in them.

Closely related to the definition of interests, of course, is the perception of threats to them, and here too there has been a distinctively American approach to the problem. The historian of the year 2086, reviewing the record of our diplomacy in the twentieth century, might very well comment on the extent to which we have allowed *forms* of government to shape our expectations about the *behavior* of government—upon our tendency to deduce intentions from organization, to assume that once we have understood the way in which another government is put together, we can derive from this a fairly good idea of what it can be expected to do.

Woodrow Wilson bears much of the responsibility for this. It was Wilson who defined our objective in entering World War I as making the world "safe for democracy"; it followed from this that Germany was our enemy because it was not democratic. Prior to our entry into World War I, Wilson's attitude toward the German government had been one of analytical detachment: he had not held Germany exclusively responsible for the outbreak of the fighting; he had been patient, some said to the point of weakness, with that country's reliance on submarine warfare; he had called, only weeks before the final rupture of diplomatic relations, for a "peace without victory." But after the United States became an active belligerent, Wilson's view shifted dramatically. He now differentiated between the German people and the German government—a distinction that was not always made during World War II—portraying the government as the embodiment of autocracy, as a regime with which one could have no dealings if one was to build the foundations for a lasting peace. He demanded its overthrow as a condition for a ceasefire. He thereby saddled the successor republican government rather than the Kaiser with responsibility for an unpopular peace; but, more than that, he created in the minds of Americans an unfortunate association between the form and the behavior of governments. He portrayed autocracy itself as the enemy, rather than the uses to which autocracy was put.

Consider, for a moment, the implications of this. The United States had coexisted throughout much of its history with autocratic governments. It would not have occurred to American statesmen in the eighteenth or early nineteenth century to say that because other states did not adhere to democratic principles—few states did at that time—there could be no common interests between them and us. Interests were thought to take precedence over ideology. Yet Wilson had now reversed that equation: henceforth ideological differences would take precedence over the existence of shared interests in the shaping of American foreign policy.

The tendency can be clearly seen in Wilson's response to the Bolshevik Revolution: he concentrated on the ideological orientation of the new Russian government—which was not only autocratic but also revolutionary—and as a result neglected the possibility that we might still share certain common interests with it, notably with regard to restraining Germany. There followed our abortive intervention, alongside our allies, in Siberia and North Russia, certainly from any viewpoint one of the least productive political-military enterprises of the century. No one can say what would have happened had we made a more careful effort to separate the interests of Lenin's government from its rhetoric; what is clear is that Lenin himself never subordinated interests to ideology, and that possibilities existed which our concentration on form rather than behavior kept us from exploring. It is ironic that in that situation we more than the Russians appear to have been the prisoners of ideology.

It is even more ironic that the United States was as slow as it was to react to the clearest example in this century of a link between form and behavior—the rise of Adolf Hitler. The delay can be explained in part by Americans' distrust of their own power; also by the fact that Europeans as well failed to grasp the significance of Hitler's movement until it was too late to prevent war. When it came, though—not long after Munich—the realization of a connection between German internal repression and external aggression burned itself deeply into our minds; it would take more than a generation to learn that not all totalitarianism carried with it the same potential for international conflict.

Curiously, the first real application of the "lessons of Munich" came, only shortly thereafter, in East Asia. Despite its ostensible commitment to the Open Door policy, the United States for four decades had witnessed, without effective protest, the expansion of Japanese power on the Asian mainland. Not until 1941, when this nation stood on the verge of war with Germany, did it take a firm stand against Japan. The reason was not, as conspiracy theorists would have it, that Roosevelt was looking for a way into the European war by the "back door"—he could have had no prior assurance that the outbreak of war with Japan would elicit a German declaration of war, as it in fact so conveniently did. Rather, it appears that we took a tough line with Japan because Munich had taught us that aggression anywhere, left unresisted, threatened the interests of stability throughout the world. We equated the Japanese effort to dominate Asia with the Nazi attempt to dominate Europe, and decided—quite apart from any rational effort to evaluate our own interests or to assess our capabilities to defend them—that we didn't like either one.

But the most egregious example of this American tendency to confuse forms of government with the behavior of governments surely has been our long-standing misunderstanding of international communism. From the onset of the Cold War until very recently—and to some extent even today—we have taken the view that adherence to the principles of Marxism-Leninism marks a government not only as internally repressive but as a threat to established international order; indeed as a puppet of Moscow itself. There was never very good evidence to support this assumption. We now know from declassified documents, for example, that even at the height of the Cold War few Soviet specialists and few informed intelligence analysts accepted the theory of monolithic communism; we know as well that as early as 1948 strategies existed within the government to take advantage of the divisive tendencies we knew to exist within the international Communist movement. A vigorous proponent of these, at least with respect to the Soviet Union and China, was no less ardent an anticommunist than John Foster Dulles himself.[3]

And yet we failed, in most cases, to apply these insights in our actual dealings with the Communist world. We blundered into a disastrous conflict with China in Korea because we interpreted that country's concern about its own security as ideologically-motivated aggression. Our failure to understand that in certain parts of the world one could be a Communist and a nationalist at the same time contributed to our even more disastrous involvement in Indochina a decade and a half later. Even to this day—and despite the fact that some of our best friends are Communists—we are still given to assuming the worst about Marxism where it appears; indeed, our fixation is so great that we tend to tolerate non-Marxist autocracies, or at least to insist upon tenuous distinctions between "authoritarian" and "totalitarian" regimes.

There is, in all of this, a curious myopia. Whether in dealing with the Kaiser's Germany, Lenin's Russia, Nazi Germany, Imperial Japan, Stalinist Russia, Communist China, North Vietnam, or with certain states in Central America and the Caribbean today, we have had a tendency to equate internal form with external action. We have assumed an "inner-directed" quality to these movements that neglects the impact of external circumstances on their behavior. We have failed to take into account the fact that, just because a nation embraces what we consider to be a repugnant ideology, it does not cease from that time forward to have state interests; those interests may, at times, diverge significantly from what ideology would appear to require. We have not had, in this century, very many national leaders who have in fact proven zealous enough to place ideological interests above state interests—indeed, Hitler himself may be the only really clear example of this. And yet we, who were so slow to recognize Hitler for what he was, have sought to make up for that failing by assuming—until otherwise convinced—ideological zealotry on the part of all adversaries since.

A balance of power need not depend upon the ideological homogeneity of the elements that make it up. Nations possessing radically different forms of government can and often do share common interests, as we repeatedly have come to find out. And yet we persist in our assumption that form governs behavior; the result has been an imprecision in the identification of threats that has caused us repeatedly to misunderstand, and to some extent to exaggerate, the challenges we have actually faced.

But what have been the consequences for the rest of the world of the way in which Americans have dealt with power, interests, and threats in the twentieth century? Here one runs into what is probably the most difficult aspect of self-evaluation: coming to grips with the results—both intended and unintended—of what one does. It involves getting into tangled questions about causation and responsibility; these are no simple matters for philosophers to handle, to say nothing of all the rest of us. It involves contemplating the counterfactual: isolating a single variable, removing it from the equation, and then looking to see what is different; this kind of thing is much easier to do in physics than in politics. Still, if we are to attain any capacity for self-judgment at all, the effect of our actions on others is one of the things we will need to learn to assess.

An exercise of this nature should proceed from the realization that the United States is neither wholly innocent of, nor wholly to blame for, the things that happen beyond its borders. The point would appear unexceptionable, and yet assumptions of both innocence and culpability have figured prominently in our approach to foreign relations over the years. For most of this century, our leaders encouraged us to believe that we were above such traditional trappings of the "old diplomacy" as power politics, or espionage, or covert action. It took revelations like Yalta, the U-2 incident, and the Bay of Pigs to alert Americans to the fact that this might not be the case; even so, the shock they manifested as late as the mid-1970s over the Church committee's exposure of CIA activities showed that the assumption of innocence still persisted. (Today, of course, "covert" operations are overtly debated and funded—or not funded.)

More recently, and among our intellectuals at least, the assumption has been one of culpability rather than innocence: the exposure of *some* instances in which power was abused has led to the suspicion that power is abused in *all* instances in which it is wielded; this in turn leads to the interesting belief that where evil exists in the world, it must be because some American put it there. Our anguished debates over our alleged involvement in the overthrow of Allende in Chile in 1973, or our alleged responsibility for the Khmer Rouge massacres after 1975, or even our alleged complicity in the maintenance of apartheid in South Africa today will clearly illustrate the point.

Our historian of the year 2086 might well say that Americans during the twentieth century were prone to a curious absolutism regarding the effects of their actions on the rest of the world: either they had no responsibility whatever for them or they were totally responsible; there seemed to be no middle ground. But of course the middle ground is where the truth lies in this case, as in so many. Americans have caused certain things to happen in the world, both good and bad, and for these we must accept responsibility. But to say, as some have implied, that a sparrow cannot fall to earth anywhere in the Third World without that event having been orchestrated by the American military-industrial-intelligence complex would appear to be stretching things a bit.

There is no way to prove that the world is better off or worse off because the United States became the dominant superpower of the twentieth century. We are hardly in a position to rerun the experiment with different variables and find out. I suspect that our historian of the year 2086 will conclude that American preeminence has had, on balance, a salutary effect, not because we have been particularly skillful or altruistic in our wielding of power, but because we have not been sinister—we have lacked the discipline for that. But one must be very cautious in attempting to anticipate historians' judgments: the track record of those given to predicting how good they were going to look in the history books has not been a particularly impressive one.

A more useful way to approach the question of consequences might be to ask what the United States has done with the power it has had. Has it in fact enhanced interests? Has it contained threats? And has it done these things in such a way as to preserve rather than degrade the quality of the international environment within which it operated?

If one defines the most vital American interest in the world as that of counteracting potentially hostile power—as indeed most American leaders have defined it—then the answer would have to be that we have been successful. Despite the fact that this has been an exceptionally violent century, aggression has not frequently paid off during it, and the United States has played an important role in bringing that about. Nor—even taking into account the position of the Soviet Union—is there a nation or group of nations on the face of the earth today capable of competing with the United States in all the categories that go to make up power. So, if maintaining a balance of power has been our interest, we must have done something right.

Threats to the balance remain, to be sure: they always will, so long as one has interests. But we have been fortunate in that the threat that posed the greatest danger—our relationship with the Russians—so far has proven to be manageable. The threats that have been more difficult to manage—revolutions, guerilla wars, terrorism—have the fortunate advantage of posing less of a danger to the international system than would an all-out war. It is the case that a new threat has emerged in its own right from the manner in which we and the Russians have handled our long-standing rivalry: the threat of nuclear war itself. But the nuclear threat is increasingly coming to be understood as an impartial one, one that endangers both the Soviet Union and the United States alike. We appear to be moving into an era of what has been called "existential deterrence," when what deters one side from attacking the other is no longer the other side's retaliatory capability, but rather the ecological consequences the use of *one's own* weapons halfway around the world might bring. For this reason—and barring the kind of accidents that are always possible in human activity—I am inclined to regard the nuclear balance as more stable than most people do, and hence, as a manageable threat.

In some ways, the greatest danger that comes from a position of world responsibility is not the one posed by one's adversaries, but the one a nation poses to itself through the ever-present temptation to misuse the power it has. One can, in the process of containing aggression, become an aggressor; one can, in the determination to resist imperialism, turn into an imperialist. How well has the United States guarded itself against these self-generated dangers?

The record, one must conclude, is mixed. Certainly we have, within our own various spheres of influence, been more tolerant of diversity than has our chief rival, the Soviet Union. There is something about the openness and flexibility of American society—and the corresponding absence of these things in Russia—that makes it easier for us to put up with imperious allies, unpredictable clients, and unruly associates. It is no accident that the Franco-American relationship survived DeGaulle, but that the Sino-Soviet relationship did not survive Mao. It is also the case that where we have set out fundamentally and as a matter of policy to restructure another society—as we did most notably in Germany and Japan after World War II—we have done so with surprising effectiveness, and with a remarkable sensitivity to the local cultures involved. It is no small accomplishment to have turned two societies upside down and still to retain the gratitude of the inhabitants for having done so.

But there is, unfortunately, a darker side to this question of how we have used our power. There have been instances where the sheer weight and mass of our presence transformed a country, even though we had intended no such effect. Where this has happened, the result has often been to our considerable disadvantage, as the examples of Cuba, Iran, and most tragically South Vietnam would surely show. Our power too often extends beyond our awareness of it, with social and political consequences that are not pleasant to contemplate.

On balance, though, the historian of the year 2086 is likely to be impressed by the number of people in today's world who would, given the choice, emulate rather than reject the American model. Whether one is talking about political institutions, economic organization, social habits, or even fast food and rock music the simple fact is that the American way of life retains great appeal—indeed, its appeal is probably growing. It is difficult for an American to account for this phenomenon, obvious though it is whenever one travels abroad. Surely it reflects no coordinated campaign on the part of the government to convey a favorable image: those who have been on the receiving end of such campaigns will have some sense of how flatfootedly ineffective they often are.

I suspect, rather, that it is precisely our lack of coordination that accounts for what is happening. The great advantage the United States has is the extent to which it accommodates diversity. It requires no great insight to take note of the fact that the world is indeed a diverse place. But it requires quite a remarkable combination of both luck and skill to maintain a political system that is comfortable with diversity at home and hence is prepared to tolerate it in the world at large: consider the number of nations that are unable to manage it. The success with which Americans have accomplished this, historians a century from now may well say, the extent to which they have been able to reconcile the appeal of spontaneity with the fact of power, may well be, more than anything else, the key to the influence they have had over the rest of the world during the twentieth century.

Discussions of national character are a risky enterprise. It was not too long ago when the British were noted for their craftiness in business, when the French were thought more adept at cooking than at government, when the Germans were regarded as authoritarian militarists, when the Japanese were known as purveyors of shoddy imitations, and when the Chinese were believed to be Marxists. Times change, for nations as for individuals. Images do not always coincide with reality, and reality at times extends beyond our capacity to understand or describe it.

And yet, there are variations in the ways nations deal with problems, as there are for individuals. What I have tried to do in this essay has been to identify some qualities characteristic of Americans and of the way they deal with foreign affairs. My list is by no means meant as a definitive catalog; certainly it should not be taken as a guide to the American character or anything approximating it. But it is an effort to initiate at least a dialogue on these matters, in the hope that if anyone is still around to listen to that history lecture in the year 2086, I will, by then, have thought of something significant to say.

NOTES

1. Daniel M. Smith, *The Great Departure: The United States and World War I, 1914–1920* (New York: Wiley, 1965).

2. Quoted in Warren F. Kimball, ed., *Churchill and Roosevelt: The Complete Correspondence* (Princeton, N.J.: Princeton University Press, 1984), 3: v.

3. See, on these points, John Lewis Gaddis, *Strategies of Containment: A Critical Appraisal of Postwar American National Security Policy* (New York: Oxford University Press, 1982), pp. 65–71, 142–43.

II B
CHARLES M. LICHENSTEIN

The better to lull Professor Gaddis into complacency, I want to begin by paying him two well-deserved tributes. The first one is broad and general: his essay is a splendid survey of a long stretch of history, full of provocative insights. It also represents a great act of courage. It's hard to know whether to congratulate or commiserate with anyone who undertakes to define the American character with some specificity; it strikes me as downright foolhardy to attempt to do this with regard to some particular area of United States policy making. So, a commendable and courageous effort indeed—or maybe "foolhardy" is the right word after all.

Obviously, the raw material is difficult to deal with. What *is* "the American character"? What, for that matter, are the principal components of policy "formation"—and, of these, which have particular salience for the formation of "foreign policy"? The raw material is ambiguous. It gives off ambivalent signals; and there is always, as in all methodological, theoretical model building, a tremendous temptation to emulate Procrustes and thus to cut and trim the evidence until, by golly, it fits the model. And vice versa.

But also, obviously, we would not be able to formulate broad hypotheses with which to assist in interpreting reality without precisely this effort of theoretical analysis, of model building. It is an important, even an essential effort—but always we must approach it with caution and a healthy measure of humility. Every time I tackle this mode of thinking I am reminded of the overriding importance—in all political anlysis, perhaps most of all in the analysis of foreign affairs—of focus on context, on the particulars, on the quite specific dynamics of each situation. For example: No, Nicaragua is not Vietnam. Central America is not Southeast Asia. Nineteen eighty-six is not 1965-to-1973. Each situation rests on its own bottom, so to speak. Each involves specific opportunities and specific obstacles. What is possible in one situation is not necessarily possible in another: United States power, United States influence, the ability of the United States to mold the real world to United States designs differ from one situation to another. Of course we can and we ought to learn from experience. But the experience itself, in all its particularity, cannot be replicated. I think the same is true from the Soviet perspective—Afghanistan is not the "Soviet Vietnam." And so I presume to offer this as Lichenstein's first and probably only law: Let us look always to the particular, as rigorously as we can, and resist the easy but imprudent generalization.

Can we in fact define—Professor Gaddis's words—"the characteristics of United States foreign policy in the twentieth century"? Is there—his words again—"a distinctive American style" in the conduct of foreign affairs? Oddly enough, and flying in the face of my own counsel of caution, I find myself responding to the evidence Professor Gaddis presents that sometimes there is less in that evidence and sometimes more to be found that is "characteristic." But most of all, my response is not so concerned whether the evidence shows more or less of a "characteristic" that Professor Gaddis identifies; rather, I draw different conclusions than he does altogether.

Consider Professor Gaddis's treatment of the problem of power. In major part, I agree with him; as Americans we have not by and large sought power (in the classical sense of seeking to wield influence in the world). We have not by and large used the power we undeniably possess to its fullest possible extent. We have never been quite comfortable in the exercise of power. Indeed Franklin Roosevelt, for example, "showed remarkable caution in not getting ahead of public opinion." But I am very much surprised that Professor Gaddis should be surprised that an American president, any American president of the modern era, would not want to get too far out in front of American public opinion. Always, it has been characteristic—and it seems to me increasingly so—of United States foreign policy that it is highly domesticated. It is not the isolated, insulated preserve of a narrow establishment elite. More and more, the substance of United States foreign policy is the object of quite broad-based public attention and public concern. For some years now this has been an element within United States policy, both in its formulation and in its implementation. And I think we see more rather than less of this public scrutiny—not entirely, let me add, to the benefit of the policy's coherence or effectiveness.

Consider the last two United States presidential elections, for example. In 1980, fully 79 percent of the Americans who voted chose "foreign policy concerns" from an open list of the factors that influenced the casting of their ballots. I recently checked a compilation of 1984 voting behavior data—cumulative polling data assembled by the editors of the magazine *Public Opinion*—and discovered that the two principal reasons given for supporting President Reagan among virtually all voting groups (by age or education or gender or socioeconomic status) were, first, strong leadership, particularly in the outside world, and second, keeping the United States strong and secure. These were the overwhelming advantages that he enjoyed in the 1984 poll—both relate directly to foreign policy concerns.

Yet, for all my agreement with Professor Gaddis about a prevailing unease among Americans with both the fact of power and our disinclination to use it to the fullest extent, I do not think he goes far enough in identifying the strength of the underlying tendency in the United States toward isolationism. It is a principal characteristic of our foreign policy today and has been throughout most of this century. Strikingly, when President Reagan was asked early in the 1984 campaign to comment on this subject, he used the word "interruption"; he said that Americans have a tendency to regard our foreign commitments as interruptions in our enjoyment of the good life. These commitments and concerns and obligations get in the way of what we would rather be doing—namely, enjoying the abundance of our land, enjoying our good fortune and the tangible benefits that most of us derive from living and working in the United States. We are a very inner-directed, a very inward-looking people. Almost everyone concedes the point for pre-World War II America—but I think that this strong underlying strain of isolationism is by no means behind us. It is very much an undercurrent, and it rises to the surface in sometimes unpredictable ways.

Moreover, this fundamental tendency to isolationism carries with it a number of other consequences, and we might want to add these to our list of characteristics of the style of United States foreign policy. I believe that most Americans are willing to use power, but only if they can be shown in advance that it has a very good chance of being effective. And they want the entire exercise to be quick and unambiguous. They are not disposed to support (and United States political leaders are not as a consequence disposed to embark on) long-term, long-haul commitments with uncertain outcomes. Let's win or lose. Let's get in and get out. Let the outcome be clear, let it be definite. And by all means let the good guys be very good and the bad guys be very bad—no doubt about which side we ought to be on. (The Grenada operation, October 1983, surely was an illustration of all that I'm here referring to; and when the operation succeeded unambiguously, it turned out that nearly everyone was for it.) In my view, all of these characteristics of the American style in foreign affairs are spin-offs of the underlying tendency to isolationism. But they are more than that, of course, and they have a profound impact on the articulation and implementation of United States foreign policy.

I do not think that I'm imagining things. Consider, as examples, recent speeches by our Secretaries of State and Defense, both of whom laid down a series of conditions governing the wise and prudent application of United States power in the world. They lay stress on such conditions as these: Make sure that the people are with you. Make sure that the application of power is more likely than not to be effective. Make the investment of power proportionate to the anticipated outcome. Do the job quickly, and do it as definitively as possible. It is interesting in this connection to think back to President Johnson's dilemma in March 1968. He did not in fact lose the New Hampshire primary at all, but he did do a lot less well than he was expected to do—and the reason was not the power of the "peace" vote, except in a very special sense. Among those who supported the "peace" candidacy of Senator McCarthy, far the greatest number (according to all survey data) were those who had lost patience with the ambiguities of the war in Vietnam, who wanted to win, and who in effect were rejecting President Johnson's strategy of slow, incremental attrition.

I believe that these are interesting and important characteristics of United States foreign policy-making. They may be aspects of a distinctive American "style" of doing business in the world.

On the concept of serving national interests, again I find myself in substantial agreement with Professor Gaddis, but I think he pushes some of his data too hard—particularly when he gets into the intricacies of the balance of power concept, and also when he specifies what he means by the typically American enchantment (my word, not his) with the parallel concept of self-determination.

To be sure, Americans tend to be uncomfortable even with the discussion of balance of power. It sounds amoral, hopelessly cynical; it signifies the descent into *realpolitik,* an alien concept imported from the corrupt Old World. At best, of course, Americans want not a balance of power but rather a preponderance of power. And, indeed, through most of our history we have enjoyed the luxury of (if we have not always effectively used) a clear preponderance of power, a mixture of military might plus massive economic and technological primacy. We may now be living in a quite unusual period of United States foreign relations in which, in some critical ways, that clear preponderance is no longer something to be assumed.

I disagree with Professor Gaddis, however, that the reduction of calculations of balance of power into a framework of national interests (which makes "us" just like "them" in that all of us simply pursue "selfish" interests) is to be quite so casually dismissed as disingenuous or even as consciously hypocritical. I do not believe that this is a fair characterization of the American style of conducting foreign policy, and mostly because of a key omission—an additional element of United States foreign policy that does indeed distinguish "us" and "them." Nowhere is the difference between Professor Gaddis and me more obvious than in our evaluations of Americans' commitment to the guiding concept of self-determination—which I regard as a wholly genuine commitment and one that is central to our foreign policy choices. What Professor Gaddis leaves out, it seems to me, or at least leaves almost subliminal, is the quite consciously and specifically moral content of United States foreign policy. I believe that most Americans ascribe a moral content to that policy, and they mean it. They expect to find it there. They judge particular policies as those policies serve or fail to serve "interests" or "purposes" that can only be described as moral. And it is this judgment as to moral content that, as I see it, helps determine Americans' commitment to foreign policy undertakings and their willingness to support certain courses of action and to stick with them for the long haul. For example, I am astonished that Professor Gaddis tends to dismiss Americans' attitudes about the Yalta agreements of 1945 as "half-hearted." Now, our leaders at Yalta may have been foolish, they may have been naive, they may even have been duplicitous (vis-à-vis their domestic constituencies as well as certain factions within the nascent leadership of liberated Eastern Europe). But I see no evidence to suggest that the American insistence on self-determination—which they profoundly believed was contained in the Yalta agreements and which was, in fact, explicitly a part of them—can accurately be described as "half-hearted."

Sometimes to the detriment of the ease with which we might implement our foreign policy (and to the making of easy choices), we do seek to preserve the reality of self-determination and to create possibilities for self-determination in whatever countries around the world where our influence can effectively be brought to bear. Under present circumstances, we particularly, of course, seek the preservation of self-determination for those who are under attack by the Soviets or their surrogates. We care about the self-determination of the Afghan people; we care about it in Chad and the Sudan and in El Salvador and, yes, in Nicaragua. I do not regard this commitment as disingenuous or hypocritical. Certainly it does not represent a retreat from reality. It is, in the perception of most Americans, an essential aspect of the real world, and I relate this perception directly to the characteristic American desire for and desire to believe that there is contained within United States foreign policy a definable, distinctive moral content.

In my judgment, much the same line of analysis applies to the genuine commitment of most Americans to the reduction or even to the eventual elimination of nuclear weapons—even as we prudently keep our powder dry in the circumstances in which presently we find ourselves. Yes, we want to reduce or eliminate nuclear arsenals. And, yes, we intend to keep our defenses and capabilities strong, and I do not see any inconsistency in holding these two positions simultaneously. Both commitments are conscious and both are deeply held by most Americans and most of our recent American governments.

Finally, a third observation about Professor Gaddis's essay. This concerns the distinction that he makes between our typical (and typically American) emphasis on "form" or "process" at the expense of "substance" or "behavior." He cites in particular the extent to which we exaggerate the continuing centrality of Marxist-Leninist doctrine in the actual behavior of the Soviet Union.

I do not think we exaggerate. Nor, for that matter, do I think that the distinction between form and behavior carries much water. In my judgment, Soviet adherence to Marxism-Leninism is real, present, dangerous—and it does make a difference to Soviet behavior. Now, I hasten to add that this, as I see it, has nothing at all to do with slipping into the affirmation of a monolithic communist bloc. Obviously, there is no such thing today as seamless, monolithic international communism. Perhaps there never has been. But equally I do not believe that the existence of a Yugoslavia or an Albania, or even a People's Republic of China, in any way (or in any really critical way) affects the nature or strategy of the Soviet Union and the preponderance of the bloc. There is, in my judgment, a Soviet bloc—maybe Soviet Empire is the more accurate term—and it does hew to a conscious, deliberate, adventurist, expansionist imperial strategy. Moreover, it seems to me that the combination of expansionism and Marxist-Leninist ideology does indeed pose a threat to established international order.

Professor Gaddis suggests that Lenin never made interests hostage to ideology. I agree. He harnessed them. He harnessed them effectively together, and I think that the present Soviet leadership continues to do so—by and large effectively. The ideology provides both impetus and rationale for Soviet adventurism and expansionism. It further lends itself, in my judgment, as a vehicle for this outward thrust—both in terms of recruiting, mobilizing, and disciplining cadres all around the world and of providing these cadres with a broadly appealing rhetoric of progress and social justice and the tide of history itself. In all these regards, I think it is far too soon to conclude that the Soviets have now moved beyond ideology—and that, in our understanding of the world and in our own approach to that world (which is to say, in our foreign policy), we too should have done with ideology and its hang-ups.

In my estimate, obviously, it is precisely the combination of ideology and interests—wielded as a powerful weapon in diverse forms of warfare—that poses a very real Soviet threat in and to the world. The threat is direct and immediate to the Afghans, the Ethiopians, the Angolans, to the people of El Salvador and Nicaragua, and most of all perhaps to the people of the bloc itself; they are the original and still the most sorely oppressed of all the victims of Marxism-Leninism. I am suggesting also that Marxist-Leninist autocracies are both qualitatively distinct from and existentially more durable than those non-Marxist autocracies which Professor Gaddis decries us for, as he puts it, tolerating. It seems to me that there are distinctions to be made—moral distinctions in major part—and that they are meaningful and critical distinctions. I think that United States foreign policy, today and typically, makes such distinctions—which is indeed a good part of its distinctiveness.

So, in the end, we doubtless must come to grips not with questions of form or style at all, but rather with the substance of United States foreign policy. My reservations over Professor Gaddis's truly noble effort to identify the characteristic style of United States foreign policy in the modern period turn mostly on issues of what that foreign policy seeks to achieve, and how and why it does so. Our debate is really over goals, and only peripherally over the ways and means of arriving at those goals.

CHAPTER III

Religious Influences on United States Foreign Policy

Introduction

The religious beliefs of the early colonists had an enormous influence on their self-understanding. They believed themselves to be blessed by God and called to develop a new and righteous society in the world. How long did these sentiments last? Do they still affect our thinking today, even if they are now unconsciously assumed or clothed in secular form? Professor Robert N. Bellah produces a rich variety of declarations from clergy, poets, and political leaders to illustrate these aspects of our cultural heritage. Such idealism can inspire exceptional efforts toward civic virtue, but if these expectations are unrealistically high, they can also produce unattractive self-righteousness, misplaced guilt, and a tendency to demonize adversaries. Are these dynamics still at work among us?

In the nineteenth century, as part of the evangelical revival called the Second Great Awakening, missionaries in large numbers were sent into the world, in particular to Asia. In addition to founding denominational churches, many of the missionaries also brought a zeal for Western-style education and sensitivity to social justice. Schools, universities, and hospitals were established and did much to transform the cultures where they were located. The formative influence of the missionaries was not restricted to foreign mission fields. Returning missionaries told their stories to their home congregations, thus shaping the understanding of many Christians about the rest of the world.

In some instances, and Dr. Bellah cites an example, American church missionary investment led to a false expectation about how nations should and would develop. Chinese revolutionary Marxism was the unexpected and unwanted offspring of the very Western values promulgated by missionaries.

Dr. Earl H. Brill identifies and illustrates three types of basic political outlooks among Americans, all of which have philosophic or religious dimensions. They are "moralistic patriotism," "idealistic humanism," and "Christian realism." Each has its merits and weaknesses.

What finally is the impact of the churches on foreign policy? Dr. Brill argues that the religious instincts of the people in the pew, not the dictates of religious institutions, are what ultimately count. The quality of American Christians' influence depends upon how well informed they are and also how sophisticated they are in judging the relevance of religious history to contemporary events. That is no small task. But prophecy has always required courage, political insight, and understanding of God's nature and goodwill.

ROBERT N. BELLAH *is the Ford Professor of Sociology and Comparative Studies, and vice-chairman of the Center for Japanese and Korean Studies at the University of California in Berkeley. He received his undergraduate degree and his doctorate from Harvard University, the latter in the fields of sociology and Far Eastern languages. For one year he was the Fulbright research grantee in Tokyo and was also the recipient of a Guggenheim fellowship from 1983 to 1984. He has published a number of books, some of which include* Beyond Belief: Essays on Religion in a Post-Traditional World *(Harper & Row, 1970),* Varieties of Civil Religion *with Philip E. Hammond (Harper & Row, 1980), and most recently* Habits of the Heart: Individualism and Commitment in American Life *(University of California Press, 1985).*

EARL H. BRILL *is presently Episcopal chaplain at Duke University in Durham, North Carolina. Dr. Brill received his undergraduate education at the University of Pennsylvania, his Th.M. from Princeton Theological Seminary, and his Ph.D. at American University. He has served as Episcopal chaplain at the University of Pennsylvania and at American University, where he also taught and chaired the American studies program. From 1974 to 1983 he was director of studies at the College of Preachers at Washington Cathedral. He is the author of a number of articles, and his books include* The Creative Edge of American Protestantism *(Seabury Press, 1966),* The Future of the American Past *(Seabury Press, 1974), and* The Christian Moral Vision *(Seabury Press, 1979).*

III A
ROBERT N. BELLAH

Religion has had a formative influence on the self-understanding of Americans, including our attitude toward foreign policy, virtually from the time the first European settlers arrived on these shores in the seventeenth century. John Winthrop's great sermon of 1630, "A Model of Christian Charity," preached on board ship before the Massachusetts Bay colonists had even landed, declared the meaning of our experiment for the world: "We shall be as a city upon a hill, the eyes of all people are upon us." Winthrop argued that our relation to the rest of the world was to be an example, indeed a "model of Christian charity," for the other nations. It is worth remembering that Winthrop was exhorting his fellow colonists to be worthy of that role. He never doubted that there was a divine calling to settle this new land. But he was not so certain that the people would be able to fulfill that calling and be worthy of the exemplary status that their calling implied.

But whatever doubts he had, he did not doubt the right of the colonists to the possession of the hill upon which they were to build their city. If the community were faithful he did not doubt that, with God's aid, "ten of us shall be able to resist a thousand of our enemies." Michael Wigglesworth, later in the seventeenth century, would refer to New England before the colonists came as

A waste and howling wilderness,
  Where none inhabited
But hellish fiends, and brutish men
  That Devils worshiped.

These devil-worshippers Wigglesworth was all too ready to identify with the Amalekites of the Old Testament:

Those curst Amalekites, that first
  Lift up their hand on high
To fight against God's Israel,
  Were ruin'd fearfully.

Thus as God's elect people the colonists were charged to bring the forces of evil under control, by military force if need be.

But this second notion, too, was from the very beginning qualified, at least in the minds of some. One of the reasons that Roger Williams was driven from the Massachusetts Bay Colony in 1637 was that he insisted the colonists were building their city on someone else's hill, to which they did not have proper title. Nor did he share the notion that the native Americans were "hellish fiends and brutish men." In verse at least as good as Wiggleworth's Williams wrote:

Boast not proud English, of thy birth and blood,
    Thy brother Indian is by birth as good.
Of one blood God made him and thee and all,
    As wise, as fair, as strong, as personal.
By nature, wrath's his portion, thine no more,
    Till grace his soul and thine restore.
Make sure thy second birth, else thou shalt see
    Heaven ope to Indians wild, but shut to thee.

So we see from the beginning two notions of America's role in the world and reservations about each of them. We were to be an exemplary people, influencing others to imitate the goodness of the society we were creating. We were to be God's avengers, bringing order to those who dared rebel against God's decrees. Yet there were doubts on both scores: whether we would really live up to our exemplary calling and whether we really were superior, in the eyes of God, to those we would control.

The vigor of the two archetypes of America's religious meaning has been extraordinary from the 1630s to the 1980s. We can still see in Ronald Reagan's second inaugural address, however lacking in literary quality it may be when compared to some of its noble predecessors, the two elements of America as an example to the nations and America as bringer of order through military might, and both as ordained by God. In the face of such an example many commentators suggest that it is long past time for America to abandon the notion of any divine mission and turn to a notion of foreign policy as based on the practical pursuit of national self-interest, the way most other nations in the world have done. With a president whose severely limited knowledge of the Bible was demonstrated recently in his misuse of a passage from the Gospel of Luke, and whose ideas about Armageddon seem calculated at moments to bring that consummation about even before God intended, that advice must seem very reasonable.

But, however reasonable, that advice is not practical. It presumes a nation other than the one in which we live. The best that we have achieved as a people, a people that really has brought hope to millions all over the world, is tied up with our sense that we are a special people, that ours is a noble experiment upon which much depends, that we are, in Lincoln's words, "the last, best hope of earth." The dangers inherent in those notions have been pointed out, as I have indicated, from the very beginning. But I would suggest that the way to meet those dangers is not to call upon us to be what we are not, to abandon our identity and our soul. The best way, and I think the only practical way, is to accept the nobility of our calling, while reminding ourselves of our unworthiness in carrying it out. The best way is to join the old conversation, attempting to advance our self-understanding, so that we may, so far as possible, purge ourselves of our arrogance and make ourselves worthy servants in the hands of God.

Perhaps our first task today is to resist the inflated rhetoric of our journalists and our high government officials about America "coming back" and "standing tall," forgetting so quickly the chastening we recently received in our role as order-bringer in the world. From the Vietnam War we learned, or I hope we learned, the terrible price in blood and treasure which must be paid in trying to bring our order to those prepared to die resisting it.

In this perennial task of deflation we have some wonderful examples from earlier in our history on which to draw. Herman Melville in the 1840s gave us the technique of ironic parody when he mimicked the fulsome rhetoric of his day:

> And we Americans are the peculiar, chosen people—the Israel of our time; we bear the ark of the liberties of the world. Seventy years ago we escaped from thrall; and, besides our first birthright—embracing one continent on earth—God has given to us, for a future inheritance, the broad domains of the political pagans, that shall yet come and lie down under the shade of our ark, without bloody hands being lifted. . . . Long enough have we been sceptics with regard to ourselves, and doubted whether, indeed, the political Messiah had come. But he has come in *us*, if we would but give utterance to his promptings. And let us always remember that with ourselves, almost for the first time in the history of the earth, national selfishness is unbounded philanthropy; for we cannot do a good to America, but we give almost to the world.[1]

At times something stronger than irony is called for. David Starr Jordan, president of Stanford during the repression of Philippine independence in the Spanish-American War, scoffed at the slogan, "The free can conquer but to save," by saying that if the American Anglo-Saxon "has a destiny incompatible with morality and which cannot be carried out in peace, if he is bound by no pledges and must ride rough-shod over the rights and wills of weaker peoples, the sooner he is exterminated the better for the world."[2]

The lesson is very apropos to us today in our involvement in El Salvador and Nicaragua where a bad situation would be worse if the irony and the scoffing had not prevented most of the American people from believing that we are supporting democratic angels against the hellish fiends and brutish men on the other side. The presence of so many

American priests and nuns in Central America, who tell a different story from that which the administration wants us to hear, has also, so far at least, done us a great service in helping us keep our heads.

So, part of our task is to keep alive the critical edge, the tradition of Roger Williams, Herman Melville, David Starr Jordan, and many others that continuously deflates our hypocritical pretensions. But the harder task is to help us clarify the way in which we can genuinely be an exemplary nation and an order-bringer in the world today. It is tempting to say, let us turn to the task of creating a good society at home as our greatest contribution to the world. Let us renounce forever our role as order-bringer to others, a role that has so often led to tragic miscalculation, injustice, and blood. There is much truth in that position and it is one that could well be argued today in the light of our recent—and current—history. Yet, finally, we cannot renounce either role. Not only have there been a few moments when we really were fighting demonic enemies in the cause of human freedom—I am old enough to have experienced World War II, when we opposed what was perhaps the most demonic regime in human history, in what Studs Terkel called "the good war"—but more importantly, we cannot now withdraw into the cultivation of our own garden, even if we wanted to. We are inextricably involved in the world, economically and politically. Often we bring disorder rather than order, suffering rather than freedom. But because of our great wealth and power we do affect every nation on earth, whether we like it or not, and it is our task to make our influence better than it has been in the past.

If religion is a part of our American culture, if religion is indelibly a part of our national self-understanding, if, as some professor has put it, there is a civil religion in America, nonetheless, the churches and other religious bodies have in their own right always played a role in helping us think about our nation and its role abroad. They have provided a variety of public theologies that sometimes reinforce and sometimes criticize our civil religion, but which to some degree independently influence our domestic and foreign policies.

There are two moments in American history when the churches have significantly spoken to our foreign policy; let us now assess their value to us today.

The first moment, if one can use that word for such a long period of time, is the moment when world mission preoccupied the American churches. It began in the early nineteenth century, at the time of the Second Great Awakening, reached a crescendo in the last decades of the nineteenth century when the Protestant churches undertook the grandiose task of the total evangelization of the world, and has proliferated in the twentieth century into all manner of interesting endeavors right up to the present, even though world mission is no longer nearly as central an idea as it was a century ago.

Although the mission enterprise has been an inherent part of Christianity since its very beginnings and has taken many forms depending on the cultures and nations from which missions have been launched, the American missionary effort in the nineteenth and twentieth centuries is unique in its sheer size and in its cultural meaning. As Winthrop Hudson has pointed out, the American missionary enterprise from the very beginning has been concerned to spread not just the gospel itself, but the peculiar blessings of American civil and religious liberty.[3] We have long been aware of the ethnocentrism involved in the missionary dream and of the contempt the early missionaries sometimes had for the cultures into which they came. The Catholic church and the major Protestant denominations have been aware of these charges and for many decades have been responding sensitively and responsibly to them. But we should not forget the exhilirated response these advocates of civil and religious liberty sometimes received. In Japan, the non-Western country I know best, many of the ablest young people flocked to the American missionaries in the 1870s and 1880s, drawing from them not only a spiritual sustenance but a reforming zeal from which many of the significant movements for civil rights and social justice in modern Japan stemmed. The story is an immense one, and much of it I do not know, but Japan is not an isolated case.

Almost from the beginning and increasingly in the twentieth century, the missionary enterprise involved not only evangelization, the planting and strengthening of new churches in lands where Christianity had seldom penetrated before, but also social service to the needs of the people, Christian and non-Christian alike. Among these services the most important over time have probably been education and medicine. American missionaries helped to found schools and colleges all over the world. Sometimes, as in Japan, the initiative came from local Christians, but American churches contributed money and teachers. In other cases the foundation effort was made by missionaries, but local teachers were enlisted so that the schools soon became part of their indigenous cultures, even while retaining their Christian distinctiveness.

Perhaps the most famous of these schools is the American University in Beirut, where such tragic events have occurred in recent months. We should remember how well that school has served the needs of the whole Middle East, how its doors were open to Muslims as well as Christians, before it was engulfed in conflicts that have brought it to the verge of extinction. I have personally visited not only the American University in Beirut but also the American University in Cairo, what was then called Roberts College near Istanbul, and a number of Christian universities in Japan such as Doshisha in Kyoto and International Christian University near Tokyo, and these are but a handful of the scores of schools in many countries to which the American missionary effort has contributed. I can testify from my own experience to the vitality of these institutions and the contribution they are making to their societies.

Similar things could be said of the dozens of hospitals that American missionaries have founded or supported all over the world. And in addition to the institution building that these efforts represent there has always been a readiness of American missionary groups to respond to critical needs such as famine or epidemic. Much of the American effort to alleviate hunger in Africa today, for example, comes under missionary auspices.

The missionary effort has deeply colored our whole attitude toward foreign policy. Particularly in the years when America maintained a low profile in the world militarily and politically, the kind of direct relationship—people to people, even person to person—that the missionaries represented seemed the right way for America to relate to the rest of the world. Both the exemplary and the order bringing aspects of our relationship to other countries were involved, but not primarily under government sponsorship. The missionaries were to be themselves exemplars of a freer, more self-confident way of living. They were to show forth in their lives not only Christian charity but democratic freedom. Inevitably many failed, but many succeeded and are remembered. With respect to order bringing, the idea was to stimulate self-help. Medicine and education were seen as strengthening the bodies and minds of those in foreign lands so that they could create enlightened and democratic societies, touched with the American model. However much the reality belies the ideal, the conception that Americans in foreign lands, American policy toward foreign nations, should be helping others to help themselves is still a powerful element in our political culture.

Just how strongly these ideas can influence our actual foreign policy can be illustrated by our relations with China during the last fifty years, a matter currently being studied by my colleague, Richard Madsen. For a long while, China was the very fulcrum of the American missionary effort. It was there that we gave the most and it was there, we thought, that we were experiencing the greatest successes. Our romance with Chiang Kai-shek was very much influenced by our idea of him as a Methodist Christian concerned to bring American-style democracy to China. Few Americans understood the hard Confucian neotraditionalism that was the real essence of his regime. When in 1949 the Chinese Communists drove Chiang Kai-shek and his Kuomintang government from the mainland—when, as Americans so revealingly put it, "we lost

China"—there was an emotional reaction in this country of almost unparalleled intensity. The sting was the sting of ingratitude, "after all we had done for them." For over thirty years we treated China like a leper, an unspeakable international monster, with which no decent person would have anything to do—far worse than we ever treated the Soviet Union before, during, or since. And yet today we are all friendly again. Americans are visiting China and Chinese are studying in America. Of course it is largely that an enemy of our enemy is our friend, but it is not only that. The Chinese are not only friendly, they are grateful. They are not only grateful, they are learning from us again. A great deal can be forgiven once the relationship returns to something close to what we consider normal. The Japanese, who were our favorites in the decades right after the war, have learned, it would seem, all too well. They are our chief competitors. We are more comfortable with those we can still instruct.

Turning now to the second moment in which the churches have spoken to our foreign policy, let me characterize it as the moment of social responsibility, which I see as growing steadily during the twentieth century, becoming prominent particularly in the last twenty years, and reaching a kind of culmination in the two recent pastoral letters from the American Catholic bishops: the Pastoral Letter on War and Peace of May 1983 and the draft Pastoral Letter on Catholic Social Teaching and the United States Economy of November 1984. I call this second moment the moment of social responsibility not because the moment of world mission was socially irresponsible, but because it was so fundamentally individualistic in its assumptions.

There is an ineradicably individualistic element in the missionary effort. One is trying to win souls, inevitably individual souls. Even when one builds institutions, such as schools and hospitals, they are institutions that contribute to society by strengthening the minds and bodies of individuals. The whole notion of foreign policy that emerges from this religious orientation emphasizes the personal relationship between peoples conceived in such terms as generosity and gratitude. The moment of social responsibility in the thinking of the churches about foreign affairs does not renounce any of the aspects of the world mission model. It adds, however, another dimension. It perceives that the relations between nations are not only personal but structural, that economic and political considerations must be taken into account that transcend assistance to individuals, however fundamental that personal aspect remains. The moment of social responsibility involves hard thinking about economic, social, and political systems, something that Americans, with our inveterate tendency to think in personal, individual terms, have difficulty doing.

The moment of social responsibility, like the moment of world mission, has exemplary and order-bringing aspects. In this view the resolution of deep structural problems of poverty and injustice in our own society must go hand in hand with our effort to bring greater justice and equity to the world system. The Pastoral Letter on War and Peace quotes Pope John Paul II in an address to American Catholics in Yankee Stadium in 1979 as saying:

> Within the framework of your national institutions and in cooperation with all your compatriots, you will also want to seek out the structural reasons which foster or cause the different forms of poverty in the world and in your own country, so that you can apply the proper remedies. You will not allow yourselves to be intimidated or discouraged by oversimplified explanations which are more ideological than scientific—explanations that try to account for a complex evil by some single cause. But neither will you recoil before the reforms—even profound ones—of attitudes and structures that may prove necessary in order to recreate over and over again the conditions needed by the disadvantaged if they are to have a fresh chance in the hard struggle of life. The poor of the United States and of the world are your brothers and sisters in Christ.[4]

The Pastoral Letter on War and Peace calls upon the church to be a community of conscience, educating its own members and reaching out to all Americans so that we can embody the principles of justice and peace in our own society and encourage their acceptance as the basis for the relation between the nations.

The draft Pastoral Letter on the Economy is, if anything, an even more remarkable document than the Pastoral Letter on War and Peace. Its first part, "Biblical and Theological Foundations," attempts to describe the Christian basis for the ethic of social responsibility in our national life and international relations, in ways most of us badly need to hear. Insisting on the primacy of human personhood and the dignity that flows from the fact that we are created "in the image and likeness of God," the letter goes on to say that

> Economic life must serve and support this dignity which needs to be realized in relationship and solidarity with others. To be human is to hear the call of community. We can find true identity only "through a sincere gift" of ourselves. Human wisdom and experience confirm this religious conviction that human life is essentially communitarian.[5]

As Americans we have often been tempted to believe that our existence as individuals is primary and that society exists only to enhance the interests of the individual. But the bishops are reminding us of the biblical teaching that our personhood is realized only in community, in relationship and solidarity with others, that "human life is essentially communitarian."[6]

The structural implications of this teaching are indeed major and do indeed call for the profound reforms to which Pope John Paul II referred. The bishops point out that "The distribution of income and wealth in the United States is so inequitable that it violates the minimum standard of distributive justice."[7] To do something about that would move very much against the political mood of the moment where entrepreneurial incentives are being offered as the answer to our economic problems. Similarly the bishops speak up for an increase in economic democracy. Quoting the Second Vatican Council to the effect that "the active participation of everyone in the running of an enterprise should be promoted," the bishops go on to say, "A new experiment in bringing democratic ideals into economic life calls for serious exploration of ways to enhance such participation."[8]

This is not the place to review in any detail the bishops' recommendations for changes in our economic life. I merely want to point out that their call for us to become more exemplary in this regard at home is intimately connected to their call for America to play a new role in overcoming the economic disparities in the world, which are many times greater than those in our own society. America must, they argue, because of our great power, exercise a decisive role in the reform of the international economic order. In this respect they quote the prophetic words of Pope John Paul II in Canada in September 1984:

> In the light of Christ's words (Matt. 25:35–36), this poor South will judge the rich North. And the poor people and poor nations—poor in different ways, not only lacking food, but also deprived of freedom and other rights—will judge those people who take these goods away from them, amassing for themselves the imperialistic monopoly of economic and political supremacy at the expense of others.[9]

Not surprisingly we are only at the beginning of this second moment of social responsibility. It is easier for us as American Christians to understand the immediate personal claim of the mission ideal, the obligation to reach out to the neighbor in need. But the social responsibility ideal teaches us that we will not be adequate to that task unless we also, as Christians, take responsibility for the structures and powers of our nation, correcting and reforming their injustices and abuses, so as to make our own society more exemplary and the world order more just.

National self-interest as a factor in our foreign policy has, in fact, never in our history been neglected, nor is it being neglected today. But we would not be true to ourselves as Americans if we were willing to leave it at that. If we would be true to our calling, we must discern what that calling entails in the difficult circumstances of today's world, and respond to it as vigorously as we can.

NOTES

1. Herman Melville, *White-Jacket*, in *Redburn, White-Jacket, Moby-Dick* (New York: The Library of America, 1983), p. 506.

2. Cited in Ralph Henry Gabriel, *The Course of American Democratic Thought* (New York: The Ronald Press, 1956), p. 385.

3. Winthrop S. Hudson, *Nationalism and Religion in America* (New York: Harper & Row, 1970), pp. 94–95.

4. National Conference of Catholic Bishops, *The Challenge of Peace: God's Promise and Our Response*, A Pastoral Letter on War and Peace, May 3, 1983 (Washington, D.C.: United States Catholic Conference, 1983), p. 81.

5. First draft, Bishops' Pastoral, "Catholic Social Teaching and the U.S. Economy," *Origins, NC Documentary Service*, November 15, 1984, p. 343.

6. Ibid.

7. Ibid., p. 340.

8. Ibid., p. 367.

9. Ibid., p. 375.

III B
EARL H. BRILL

Professor Bellah has offered a concise account and a compelling vision of religious themes that recur again and again in our national history. I certainly agree on the centrality of those themes: America as exemplar and America as bringer-of-order, with all of the ambiguity involved in their attempted realization. And Professor Bellah is surely right to see that the issue of human solidarity, the recognition of the reality of world community, ought to be at the heart of the agenda of Christians who seek to influence the foreign policy of the United States.

Having no major disagreement with Professor Bellah's analysis, I would like to examine some other aspects of the relationship of religion to foreign policy. The first is the question of what influence religion has on our foreign policy. The second has to do with what kind of religious orientation favors what kind of foreign policy.

With regard to the first issue, I think we can all agree that it is very difficult to trace religious influences on foreign policy for a number of reasons. In analyzing the roots of any policy choice, a number of variables have to be taken into account: economic and political considerations, ideological presuppositions, national and ethnic influences, among others. Religion is but one strand in a very complex fabric of forces that go into the making of policy.

Then too, religious influences tend to be indirect. Church and synagogue have been instrumental in producing statesmen of character and conviction who have frequently brought the deepest values and commitments of their religious tradition to the work of policy making. While the results of their work may not always show the direct effect of their religious orientation, those religious convictions often play a part, however incidental and even unconscious, in their outlook and consequently in their policy choices.

Franklin Roosevelt illustrates both of these factors. When asked about his political philosophy, he looked blank for a moment and then replied, "I am a Christian and a Democrat." Surely that Christian commitment showed itself in his genuinely humanitarian outlook, but it does not always show up as clearly in particular policy choices. And we have no reason to expect that it would, for it was inevitably and inextricably linked with his political instincts, his national loyalty as an American and his loyalty to the English heritage that was so important to the self-understanding of the American upper class. In Roosevelt's case, the religious influence was undeniably there, but it was likely to be expressed only indirectly. The same can be said about many other American statesmen. I would concur, then, with Professor Bellah that religion has had a formative influence on our self-understanding but, I would add, very little direct effect on policy.

Another difficulty in identifying religious influences is that they often appear where they are not. Given the vaguely Christian orientation of the general public, politicians are often tempted to offer moral, ethical, or religious justification for policies that have been arrived at on quite other grounds. Professor Bellah has referred to President Reagan's recent allusion to Luke 14:31–32 in support of his plan to continue the enormous increases in military spending. Now you may believe that Reagan sat down with his Bible, studied St. Luke's Gospel and then, after careful and prayerful meditation on the text, decided that it impelled him to increase spending for the military, but I am inclined to doubt it.

Our consideration of religious influences on foreign affairs is further complicated by the great diversity of perspectives in the American religious community. That variety raises my second question: What kind of religion favors what kind of foreign policy?

We can identify three basic outlooks that lead to widely differing religious influences on foreign policy. The first, which I will call "moralistic patriotism," often has a touch of manichean dualism mixed in with it. That is, it tends to see the world in terms of sharp contrasts of good and evil, black hats and white hats. Our guys, of course, wear the white hats. Our guerillas are freedom-fighters; their guerillas are terrorists.

Moralistic patriotism is often associated with evangelical Protestantism, which has a clear and simple moral code: this country has been good to you. Its authority commands respect and loyalty. America's role in the world is to advance the cause of freedom. To be a good Christian is to be a good American. The bringer-of-order tradition that Professor Bellah described is a part of this view. It leads to the conviction that this nation has been chosen by God to bring to the rest of the world the benefits of Christianity, democracy, and the capitalist system.

This outlook has had both liberal and conservative proponents. Woodrow Wilson, sounding more like a Calvinist lay preacher than a politician, proudly proclaimed in 1913 that the United States would henceforth refuse to recognize governments that had achieved power through force and violence—a curious position, given the origins of our own government. I might also note how often the term "crusade" has been used to describe our actions in the world. Then of course we have seen how the Cold War has so often been interpreted in moral and religious terms, that is, as a struggle to prevent the spread of militant atheistic communism throughout the world.

In 1935 sociologist Ray H. Abrams analyzed the role of the American churches in the first World War in a devastating little book called *Preachers Present Arms.*[1] He pointed out that in that war, as in all American wars, the clergy leaped to the support of the state, vilifying the enemy in the most extreme and violent language and appealing to their flocks to destroy the Huns to save Western civilization from barbarism. Abrams makes his case by including enough direct quotation to make the disinterested bystander's hair stand on end.

And at the risk of incurring another libel suit, I might add that, much more recently, General Westmoreland is said to have called the Vietnam fiasco "Christ's war."[2] During that tragic time, even more moderate voices were willing to claim that, in the words of one prominent preacher, "We do have the right to be in Vietnam. We have more than the right. We have a moral obligation."[3]

The emergence of evangelical Christians on the political scene in recent years has added strength and plausibility to this way of thinking about foreign affairs. Indeed, it has led to a significant revival of the American world mission theme that Professor Bellah associates with the nineteenth century. Just a few years ago, I asked a local leader of the Moral Majority how he was able to reason from his announced position as a biblical literalist to the organization's view that the United States should build up its military forces and prepare to fight communism in every corner of the globe. His response was that we had to do it to protect our missionaries overseas.

The reaction against this way of thinking led to almost the opposite religious perspective on world affairs. We might call this the "idealistic-humanitarian" approach, because it tends to judge foreign policy by universal moral standards. Thus the goals of foreign policy should be the Christian virtues of peace, justice, equality, human rights, and the rule of law. Foreign governments are judged to be good or evil according to their commitment to these values. American policy should support the good and dissociate from the evil. Dictators are generally condemned and revolutions of the people supported.

This position frequently finds itself in opposition to actual policies of the United States government. At its most extreme form, it has sometimes tended toward pacifism, and many people with this perspective opposed our entry into the second World War. Since then, its commitment has been to internationalism, especially as exemplified by the United Nations and its associated organizations. It urges multilateral rather than unilateral approaches to world problems, political and diplomatic efforts rather than military solutions, economic aid rather than military assistance. Proponents of this view would affirm the tradition that Professor Bellah has described as America the exemplar to the world.

The idealistic-humanitarian perspective has been condemned and even ridiculed for being naive and impractical. And it does, indeed, tend to place an unrealistically high estimate on humanity, overlooking our only-too-human propensity for sheer cussedness. It sometimes fails to distinguish the good from the attainable and to underestimate the complexities of power politics. It sometimes ignores the demonstrable fact that revolutions of the people can turn out to be as violent and repressive as the regimes they overthrow.

At its worst, then, this position can place unrealistic demands upon the working statesman. But at its best, it keeps before the nation the inescapable ethical component of foreign policy, without which our actions in the world could easily descend to the exercise of naked force in the service of the most cynical conception of national self-interest.

The idealistic tradition inevitably produced its own negation in the work of Reinhold Niebuhr, who provided the classic critique of that position. As we all know, I am sure, Niebuhr advocated, as an alternative, what has become known as "Christian realism," a view that recognizes the inevitability of evil consequences arising from our best efforts at making political choices. In situations in which "the right thing to do" is simply not on the agenda as a possibility, Niebuhr taught, the political actor must make a decision from among the alternatives actually available and be willing to take responsibility for achieving proximate gains and for any evil consequences that might ensue.

Niebuhr's thought is too well known to require any elaboration here, but suffice it to say that he was a complex and conscientious thinker who was constantly aware of the hazards implicit in his thought. It is one thing to justify doing some damage incidentally in the pursuit of a good and responsible policy. That can be called regrettable necessity. It is quite another thing to justify any damage that results from one's policy choices. Niebuhr never fell victim to that delusion, but many of his lesser disciples did.

Some of the "best and the brightest" who gave us Vietnam would have been glad to enlist under the Christian realist banner, or at least to have signed on as "atheists for Niebuhr." For many of them, communism came close to being the one absolute evil and anticommunism so important a cause as to justify subversion, espionage, dirty tricks, lying to the public, and even assassination. Our military intervention in Vietnam was interpreted as an exercise of moral responsibility that would ultimately produce good results, despite the regrettable but necessary suffering that was produced along the way. I think that Senator Fulbright may have erred in calling our policy the arrogance of power. He might better have called it the arrogance of responsibility. It is instructive, by the way, to note that the original leaders of the realist group—Niebuhr, Hans Morgenthau, and George F. Kennan—all opposed the war in Vietnam on realistic grounds. It was their less thoughtful disciples who allowed themselves to get caught up in supporting it.

One of the better known of these disciples is Ernest F. Lefever, whose early book, *Ethics and United States Foreign Policy,* carried an approving comment from Niebuhr and a foreword by Morgenthau.[4] Its ethical stance was certainly in the realistic mode, but it was primarily an attack on those soft-headed religious idealists who were unequipped to deal with serious issues in the real world. One can already see in this work a line of thinking that would later lead him to act as apologist for the presumably realistic policies of the South African government, but make it impossible for him to be a credible advocate of human rights on behalf of the United States.

In making this point, I do not intend to single out Lefever for criticism, but rather to use his career to demonstrate the fact that the realist position, like all the others, has its own peculiar hazards. Each of these positions has, as they say, the defects of its qualities. The first easily leads to national self-righteousness and to the support by the religious community of any foreign policy that an incumbent administration chooses to adopt. The second is prone to harbor unrealistic expectations and to advocate courses that could lead to disaster, even though they may proceed from the most morally pure motives. The third can lead to justification of the most unjustifiable policies in the name of regrettable necessity and the assumption of awesome responsibility.

Today, religion may have its greatest impact on foreign policy when it contributes to the building of an informed and responsible public opinion. There is considerable disagreement over just how much influence public opinion now has on the making of foreign policy. Those engaging in formulating policy usually say that it has a powerful influence, but those trying to influence policy from the outside feel that public opinion has little effect. At the very least, I suspect that public opinion does set some moral limits on the activity of government. We did not, for example, bomb North Vietnam "back to the stone age," as one of our generals advocated. Perhaps the recent statements of the Roman Catholic bishops on nuclear war and economic justice will have their greatest effect, not by what they say to the government directly, but by what they say to the church, that is, by contributing to the creation of a better informed and morally sensitive public.

That is an especially important function in these days, when foreign policy is made by the national administration and then sold to a poorly informed public through the use of inflamed rhetoric and specious moralizing. In such a situation, any religious perspective can become grist for the government's public relations mill. As Edward Gibbon put it, speaking of ancient Rome,

> The various modes of worship which prevailed in the Roman world were all considered by the people as equally true; by the philosopher as equally false; and by the magistrate as equally useful.[5]

A reading of today's newspaper will indicate that things have not changed much. The present administration, in pursuing its hard-line policies in Latin America and with respect to the Soviet Union, can expect automatic, even enthusiastic support from the moralistic patriots and opposition from the humanitarian idealists. The realists, as usual, are skeptical but open to persuasion.

If you would like a test case for the influence of religion on foreign policy, I suggest you look at Latin America. Professor Bellah has observed that we have, in our policy toward Nicaragua, a head-to-head collision between a militantly anticommunist administration which insists on seeing Nicaragua's internal struggle as an East-West confrontation and a religious community which includes many clergy and lay people who have actually lived and served in Nicaragua and thousands more who have visited there over the past two years to see things for themselves. Those two groups have quite opposite views of the Nicaraguan revolution. So far this sector of the religious community has had little impact on our policy toward Nicaragua. Should the Reagan administration agree to discontinue aid to the contras and cease the implied threats of direct action, that could be seen as a major triumph of an informed and committed religious group. The future of American policy in that one small country will be an index of just how much an aroused religious community can affect a policy in which politicians and cold warriors have a major investment.

Finally, I do not think that the religious community is, or need be, totally lacking in influence on American foreign policy. The experience of the American Jewish community in demanding support for Israel illustrates the possibilities inherent in organizing a committed and vocal constituency. The churches and synagogues of America contain a great untapped reservoir of energy, commitment, and ethical concern. The question is how to tap that reservoir. The religious right seems to have begun to do just that. It is time for the rest of the religious community to bring a different kind of agenda to bear on our foreign policy.

As I go about the church—and not just my own church—I am appalled by the relative lack of ongoing discussion around the kinds of issues being discussed in this volume. Church programs still focus largely on the interior life and on moral concerns that affect the individual or, at most, the family and neighborhood. World affairs seldom make the ecclesiastical agenda.

Yet if the religious community is to have any influence on foreign policy, it will be because politicians are made to see religion as a force with which to reckon. That can happen only as men and women in congregations throughout the land become informed, convinced, and energized around issues in which religious people have a stake. Official reports, convention resolutions, and public statements have little effect. Only an aroused public opinion will have any effect on those who make and execute foreign policy. The Catholic bishops' statements offer the kind of leadership that can inform the religious community and help to shape a public opinion that the political world will have to take seriously. If local congregations begin to respond to that kind of leadership by engaging in thoughtful ethical discourse around issues in world affairs, it may be possible for the forces of religion to have a genuinely creative and responsible impact upon American foreign policy.

NOTES

1. New York: Round Table Press, 1935.

2. George R. Davis, "The Vietnam War: A Christian Perspective," in Michael P. Hamilton, ed., *The Vietnam War: Christian Perspectives* (Grand Rapids: Eerdmans, 1967), p. 48.

3. Ibid., p. 55.

4. Cleveland: Meridian Books, 1957.

5. Cited in Daniel J. Boorstin, *The Genius of American Politics* (Chicago: University of Chicago Press, 1953), p. 135.

CHAPTER IV

Profits at What Cost? America in the World Economy

Introduction

At this point the focus of the book moves from a primarily historical analysis to a commentary on contemporary aspects of foreign policy. From the very beginnings of our nation, when the desire for trade overcame the early settlers' wish to build an isolated Eden in America, economic needs have had a profound effect upon our international policies. Such material self-interest is an offense to those who aspire to idealistic forms of patriotism and hence is often unacknowledged. Richard J. Barnet has no such inhibitions, and with honesty and clarity he identifies our self-delusions. "Nothing seems to work quite as it is supposed to work," he says. With that introduction, he proceeds to analyze the economic health of the nation state, the ambivalent role of multinational corporations, and changes in United States employment patterns.

In the last two decades important and disturbing structural changes have taken place in the United States economy, partly as a result of technological development but also because of the wealth of cheap labor for industry in the Third World. Mr. Barnet discusses these and related issues and concludes with some suggestions for their amelioration.

Dale R. Weigel, in response to Mr. Barnet, examines the role of the international economy with special reference to the growing influence of the free market. He supports the moderating influence of the World Bank and the International Monetary Fund and their ability to promote economic development in the poorer countries. These points help to reinforce our need to be concerned for the welfare of both economically weak and strong nations.

RICHARD J. BARNET *is a senior fellow of the Institute for Policy Studies, an independent center in Washington, D.C., devoted to research on public policy issues. During President Kennedy's administration he was an official of the State Department, the Arms Control and Disarmament Agency, and a consultant to the Department of Defense. He is a graduate of Harvard College and Harvard Law School, and has been a frequent lecturer and visiting professor at universities in the United States and overseas. The subjects to which he has devoted most of his attention are issues of war and peace, economic aspects of nuclear armament, the work of multinational corporations, and international economic alliances. Some of his books include* Who Wants Disarmament? *(Beacon Press, 1960),* The Lean Years: Politics in the Age of Scarcity *(Simon and Schuster, 1980),* The Alliance: America, Europe, Japan. Makers of the Postwar World *(Simon and Schuster, 1981). His essays are widely published in journals both in this country and abroad.*

DALE R. WEIGEL *has been chief of the Financial Policy and Planning Division in the World Bank since May 1983. Prior to that he spent ten years in the International Finance Corporation as manager of the economics staff and, subsequently, manager of the promotion staff. He was an associate professor at the University of Iowa, and he worked as an international economist for the United States Agency for International Development during 1966–1968. Dr. Weigel was educated at Carnegie-Mellon University and Stanford University where he earned his Ph.D. from the Graduate School of Business in 1966.*

IV A
RICHARD J. BARNET

Politicians in the United States have made it almost a rite of passage to denounce government as a prime source of social ills and to celebrate the free market as the key to social progress. The nostalgic rhetoric of the Reagan Revolution—the freer that capitalists are to pursue their economic self-interest the better off everyone will be—is an understandable, perhaps inevitable, reaction of the 1980s to the successes and disappointments of the 1960s and 1970s. But it is ironic that the credo of Herbert Spencer and William McKinley should be revived with such zeal at precisely the moment when the major ideological currents of the twentieth century are all in crisis. In the United States, politicians speak worshipfully of the miracle of the "free market," sounding much like the Wizard of Oz administering courage to the cowardly lion.

Yet the credo of the marketplace neither describes the actual economic system in the United States nor does it offer solutions to the basic social and economic problems of the nation which, the recent cylical recovery aside, seem remarkably resistant to ideological fervor. Adam Smith would have difficulty recognizing as old-fashioned capitalism an economy that subsidizes its farmers to the tune of $30 billion or more and writes an annual "corporate welfare check" of $140 billion, as the *Wall Street Journal* editorial staff writer Gregory Fossedal puts it. Not exactly a bastion of rugged individualism.

Adam Smith was too shrewd a social observer to confuse a system which encourages concentration, bigness, and speculation with the system he envisioned. I doubt whether he would have taken aggregate growth in economic activity as unalloyed good news, as we do, regardless of the character of that growth. He might even have put the billions generated each year by the cancer economy and the automobile accident industry on the minus rather than the plus side of the ledger. He would not have clung to the illusion, in the face of mounting evidence, that encouraging the rich to enrich themselves further necessarily generates investment capital for needed services, for the restoration of ravaged cities and regions, or for the creation of economic opportunities for those growing numbers who are excluded from participation in society as producers. The effect of increasing corporate subsidies through tax breaks or of siphoning 14 percent of the federal budget into interest payments to banks, institutions, and wealthy individuals is indeed to make more money available to private investors, but the incentives to invest those funds in obvious, urgent development needs are notably absent. For example, the technology exists to create a vaccine that could wipe out malaria as smallpox was wiped out a decade ago. It is not being developed because the men, women, and children in Third World countries who get malaria are not promising customers. So the market sucks up capital for other purposes that promise a quick return. "Right now," says the investment banker Felix Rohatyn, "everybody is speculating at a level I haven't seen in forty years of business."

The ideology of command economies is not holding up well either. Ideological advertising has always been a fixture of the Communist system. The dogmas of central planning and state control are still offered as science, but in the Soviet Union the fervor is noticeably absent, and in Hungary pragmatic politicians are "capitalist roaders" of one sort or another. In China, where that epithet was invented, capitalist roaders abound and Maoism is being stood on its head. It appears that declaring the human urge to acquire property a sin and market transactions a crime is even less a prescription for solving the problems of modern society than market worship. There is much rejoicing among the ideologues of the West about the failures of the ideologues of the East, but the failures, real as they are, do not presage either imminent collapse of the Communist world nor its miraculous transformation into Jeffersonian democracy.

The more moderate alternative ideologies also seem to be in distress. Social democracy, once thought of as a promising "middle way" to steer between the inequities of buccaneer capitalism and the tyrannies of command economies, is under a squeeze generated by slow economic growth and the staggering costs of the welfare state. Increasingly, the legitimacy of each ideological system is defended not so much by its own record but by the failures of competing ideologies. In the United States it is now ritualistically asserted that the welfare state is a failure and that Europe's experiments, since Bismark's time, with social security, employment security, and the delivery of health care prove the inevitability of failure. Government cannot and should not create employment. Prosperity is inevitably undermined by policies that benefit the poor who, according to George Gilder, resurrecting Herbert Spencer, need the spur of their own poverty. Much of the hyperbolic self-congratulation we hear so much today about resurgent capitalism in the United States rests on a recital of the failures of communism and the crisis of social democracy.

Every nation across the ideological spectrum is thus experiencing enormous difficulty in squaring its ideology and public policies with the basic values which distinguish it as a community. Why this should be so is worth pondering. I would suggest one important reason is that the institution of the nation-state, whatever its ideology, is in crisis. It is unable to perform its two most important historic functions. In the nuclear age no state, however powerful, can defend its own people. What is called "defense" is a form of psychological warfare, a complex system for dramatizing the global suicide pact that goes by the name of deterrence. If the system fails, and it is becoming increasingly plausible that it will fail, no defense in the physical sense is possible. Even the most enthusiastic advocates of the Strategic Defense Initiative do not claim 100 percent effectiveness for this expensive illusion. It is already clear that "star wars" is really a system to protect weapons, not people. So the illusion of defense is purchased by a spending race—a new sort of potlatch in which contesting leaders compete to show their greater resolution to sacrifice the well-being of their people for weapons, betting that the race will bankrupt the foe before their own economy is destroyed.

The second historic task of the modern state is to promote a stable economy and an environment conducive to civil peace within its own frontiers. This is now increasingly difficult because every nation, whatever its political orientation, is becoming more and more integrated into a world economy which is under the control neither of governments nor international authorities. The process of integration has been accelerating almost everywhere. Fifteen years ago China and the Soviet Union were militant autarchies. In the 1970s the Soviets increased their dependence on foreign trade, notably with Western Europe. The Chinese are building free trade zones of the sort they derided not so long ago as imperialist enclaves of the multinational corporation. The United States is roughly twice as dependent upon world trade as it was ten years ago. The comfortable cant of the market worshippers is that the invisible hand is at work on a global scale ushering in a new era of world prosperity. The bumps in the road—continents on the edge of starvation, massive unemployment in so-called developing countries, more than $800 billion worth of debt owed to banks and governments by countries that cannot pay it, a deindustrialization of the United States and other advanced economies in which the new "service" economy is premised on permanent high unemployment—are adjustment problems. In Schumpeter's phrase, progress is a process of "creative destruction." The invisible hand will be around before long to smooth out the bumps.

The market worshippers produce a recovery with a massive dose of federal spending—much of it for the military—and generate deficits that would have unnerved John Maynard Keynes. The United States recovers from the third recession in six years, seemingly stronger than the other industrial countries. Yet the nation has a serious trade imbalance. In 1985, the trade deficit soared to $148 billion, the highest in history. Once the world's greatest industrial nation, the United States last year imported 25 percent of its machinery. The increasing integration of the United States into a rapidly changing world economy is producing problems which market worship seems only to make worse.

The heart of the matter is the model of development now pursued in the major countries of the world. This model is to a large extent the product of a system of incentives operating on the multinational corporation, the most dynamic actor in the process of global economic integration.

Let us look at some of the characteristics of that model. The first is division of labor. The multinational corporation is the first human institution with the vision, technology, and experience to plan on a global scale. For maximizing global profit, it breaks the production process into its components and locates each part where it will contribute most to the bottom line. Thus in the electronics industry circuits are printed on silicon wafers and tested in California; wafers are then shipped to Asia where they are cut into tiny chips and bonded to circuit boards. Final assembly for video games, military equipment, and the like is usually in the United States.

The result has been a structural change in the United States economy. Between 1978 and 1982, according to the MIT economists Bennett Harrison and Barry Bluestone, 900,000 jobs were lost every year due to plant closures. To be sure the total number of manufacturing jobs grew in those years—77,000 more than were lost in the same period—but the number of people looking for work grew by almost eight million. The number of jobs for "production workers" fell by 5 percent in the 1970s while the number of managerial and supervisory positions increased—and low-paid "service" jobs grew at a phenomenal rate. The McDonald's economy—industries that pay workers an average of less than $12,500 a year—is showing the most dynamic growth in employment possibilities for Americans. (McDonald's itself is now a larger employer than United States Steel.) Between 1969 and 1982 more than two-thirds of all new jobs were in lower-wage industries. In 1969 61 percent of all jobs were in what labor statisticians designate as "middle-wage occupations"; by 1982 the percentage had fallen to 51 percent, and this trend is projected to continue until the end of the century. As a consequence of closing plants to invest more profitably elsewhere, sending out components to be processed abroad, labor-dispensing technological advances, imports—in many cases from plants owned by United States based corporations—the United States is experiencing increasingly uneven development. Thus within seven years Michigan loses 17 percent of its manufacturing base and Texas increases its manufacturing base by 32 percent. These dramatic changes bring with them serious social and political consequences which have not been addressed. Fashionable ideology says that we shouldn't even try to plan so that those who benefit from "creative destruction" share the burden and those who are the victims of the process are not abandoned.

One important consequence of the change in the global labor market is a change in bargaining power between public and private authorities. Corporations are able legally to move in and out of communities whenever business considerations dictate. Plants making small profits are closed so that money can be reinvested elsewhere at greater profit. Cities compete to attract or to keep jobs and so offer corporations tax breaks and other incentives which shift the cost of services to those least able to bear them. The shift in bargaining power has contributed to the fiscal crisis of cities.

Another consequence is the decline of labor's bargaining power. The decline of the American labor movement—less than 20 percent of the work force is now organized—has accelerated the downward pressure on wages and the increasing lack of legal and financial protection for American workers. Because of the mobility of capital and the relative immobility of workers, unions have had to make wage concessions to keep plants from moving. Even the threat to move has a disciplining effect on the labor force. Neither regions, such as the industrial Midwest where the effects of deindustrialization are disproportionately felt, nor individuals abandoned by corporations in the continuing shift of production have the political power to protect themselves.

There is a conventional Panglossian view of all this which is now popular in an era when it is fashionable to deride "doomsayers." Have a little more faith in the market and it will rescue us by neatly rearranging the world. The dirty smokestack jobs are leaving the country and are being replaced by clean high-tech jobs and the burgeoning service industry. At the same time the nasty jobs are going to the poor countries where people desperately need them and are happy to do them. Why are you shaking your fist at progress?

The problem is that people, unlike statistics, have roots. It may warm the heart of a Youngstown steelworker to read of two fine jobs in California or ten jobs in Taiwan financed by the disinvestment in his own city—but it will not put food in his stomach. For auto workers, steelworkers, rubber workers, and textile workers in depressed areas with unsellable houses, huge mortgages, and kids in school it is not so easy to graze far from home. Attracting high-technology jobs to depressed areas is often touted as the answer to the employment problem in the United States. But the facts do not support the optimism. According to the

Bureau of Labor Statistics not more than 7 or 8 percent of new jobs will be in high technology. Most of these jobs are not highly paid. Thus a steelworker makes twelve to fifteen dollars an hour; many computer operators make little more than the minimum wage. The majority of these new jobs are not only low paid but they are, in the words of Arthur Shostak, a labor authority at Drexel Institute, "incredibly mind-stunting, mind-dulling." The automation process renders menial many operations that used to require considerable skill, that used to give workers pride and a certain job security.

Shifting from older-type jobs to the new service-oriented, high-tech economy involves substantial losses for workers. Almost half of the several hundred thousand auto workers who were laid off in the recent recession never got their jobs back. Those who did find new jobs, according to a survey of the Social Welfare Research Institute at Boston College, had to take a 30 percent pay cut. Forty-one percent of them no longer have employer-paid health insurance. Most have no pension. This is just one example of a widespread phenomenon which Harrison and Bluestone call "skidding out of the middle class."

Most of these "service" jobs, which increasingly are being filled by women, are menial, insecure, and poorly paid. The phenomenal creation of new jobs in the United States economy and the rise of a new labor market is to a considerable extent a response to poverty. Families need two incomes to survive. Women can be underpaid because they are not perceived as responsible heads of household but as auxiliary wage-earners. For every woman who enters the job market to find fulfillment and meaning there are many more who would prefer not to sweep other people's floors or sit all day in front of a machine but who need the paycheck. The traditional Keynesian remedies for stimulating aggregate demand do not address the problems of structural unemployment. The undereducated, the poorly educated, the targets of discrimination represent even more of a structural problem. More than 40 percent of black teenagers on the eastern seaboard are unemployed and seemingly unemployable.

Yes, that is regrettable, it is said. But if we spend a little less on such people for their education, preventive health care, job training, and decent housing, they will become more realistic about what is in store for them and they will flock more enthusiastically into the McDonald's economy. The judicious administration of humiliation, which is a hallmark of the welfare system, protects poor people from the dangerous illusion of the free lunch. Hunger concentrates the mind and encourages the indolent to more heroic efforts to find work.

Meanwhile, the hard-working people of Asia, Africa, and Latin America are benefitting from foreign investment by United States based multinational corporations. According to the credo of the market, corporations almost invariably do good by doing well. To suggest otherwise is to be "antibusiness" or to be looking for villains. The role of multinationals, or transnationals as they are more frequently called these days, in poor countries is a mixed picture. The issue is not virtue or villainy. It is whether in particular cases the multinationals, by responding to the incentives created by the market as modified by governments, are producing stable development and progress or are, whatever their intentions, contributing to uneven development and poverty.

Jobs are created by the multinationals in the Third World, but they are open to only a small fraction of the population, and to a great extent the jobs are not secure. Throughout Asia, Africa, and Latin America, including more than one hundred free trade zones which offer special labor, tax, and other concessions to multinationals, millions are being employed. In South Korea, for example, a woman typically earns three to five dollars a day for assembly work for which a female worker in the United States would earn an equivalent sum in an hour. The work week is often fifty-five to sixty hours. Young women between sixteen and twenty-five are preferred for an overseas labor force recruited primarily for monotonous, repetitive assembly operations. Because the work adversely affects health, especially the eyes, there is rapid turnover. As one personnel manager in an assembly plant in Taiwan put it, "Young male workers are too restless and impatient to be doing monotonous work with no career value. If displeased, they sabotage the machines and even threaten the foreman. But girls, at most they cry a little."

As the wave of industrialization has swept across parts of the Third World, people have been forced off the land because they cannot afford to stay there as alternative uses—industrialization or mechanized agriculture for export—become more profitable. Thus millions who once were outside the money economy are now in it—but without money or the prospect of a job. The industrial jobs offered by the multinationals, as dreary as they are, are obviously welcomed by those without alternatives. But they are not secure. During the 1974–75 recession, half of the forty thousand workers in Mexico who work in the industrial zone along the United States border were laid off. One of the attractions of "foreign sourcing" of labor in such places as the Philippines is the guarantee of freedom from militant labor organizations by governments prepared to sacrifice health, safety, and decent working conditions for their people for the sake of the national compulsion to export.

The impact of foreign investment in poor countries depends, as it does in this country, on the bargaining power of those who must deal with the multinational corporations. Their interest is to pay the lowest wages and to have as few restrictions imposed by the local government as possible. The clearer local government is about the model of development it wishes to pursue the more likely the foreign investment will be beneficial. The more alternatives the host country has in either competing private funds or public capital the better bargain it can strike. But the fact remains that the most urgent development needs of poor countries—health care, sanitation, water, literacy programs and schooling, and food production for local consumption—are not profitable and will not attract multinationals.

So the celebrators of the market advise poor countries that they can generate the capital themselves to develop through exports. The increasingly heavy reliance on exports is a striking characteristic of the development model dominated by the multinational corporations. Between 1973 and 1980 the value of world industrial production increased two and a half times, but world trade increased more than four and a half times. Every country, it seems, has adopted the slogan "Export or Die." The power of the multinational corporation rests in large measure on its proven ability to generate exports. Tax and other incentives offered by governments to multinationals encourage exports rather than the development of a domestic market. The international consumption community is obviously a much larger market than any national market. The United States tariff law now encourages American corporations to locate facilities outside the United States for export to the United States.

What is the matter with such great export dependence? What is wrong with using what economists call "comparative advantage" to maximize the world flow of goods and services? If South Korea has a comparative advantage in a seemingly inexhaustible supply of young women with good eyesight and nimble fingers, why shouldn't the country gain precious foreign exchange by encouraging a substantial part of its labor force to attach itself to the global export economy? If the United States, following the pattern traditionally associated with underdeveloped countries, exports food and imports consumer goods and industrial machinery, what's wrong with that? The implications are not subjected to political debate, not in the United States, much less in South Korea. These implications include the gulf between workers in the better paid export economy and those in the stagnating domestic economy, the effect of using the brightest and most energetic workers to make goods for export instead of developing a domestic market, diverting scarce resources such as electric power from rural development to subsidize the manufacture of exported goods, the use of United States agriculture as an export machine creating food dependence in poor countries, and depleting the topsoil of the world's largest granary at a rate that alarms anyone who looks at the problem. The prevailing assumption is that all these developments are natural phenomena like changes of the seasons instead of the product of thousands of planning decisions in corporations and governments for which the planners are not accountable. It is an ideological myth that only public authorities plan. Multinational corporations pursue strategies of self-interest. That is precisely what they are supposed to do. But the problem is that these private planning decisions have public consequences which are not acknowledged in our political process, much less addressed.

But the uneven development that afflicts societies heavily dependent on exports is one of the problems of success. It is something to worry about if the volume of world exports continues to grow. But in recent years world trade has been almost at a standstill. Last year it picked up a bit. But what will happen in the next recession? Countries are feverishly trying to export the same mix of goods to the same people. The world population grows, but in the recent period of economic stagnation the market for exported goods has not grown at anything like the rate it did during the unprecedented and, I believe, unrepeatable bonanza years between 1950 and 1970. Under the pressures of austerity, more people seem to be leaving the international consumption community than are entering it. The pressures to export have led to quotas, protectionist rhetoric (and some increase in protectionism), and an outright rejection of proposals to open the markets of the developed world to the developing nations and to reduce the growing gap between what they must pay to import machinery and consumer goods and what they earn from the sale of their agricultural products. The older industrial nations, particularly in Europe, are increasingly worried about the competition from the new export machines in the South Koreas and Taiwans.

The trade standoff is compounded by the debt problem. The development model of the multinationals has been based on lavish debt. It is not coincidental that the "miracle economies" of the 1960s, notably Mexico and Brazil, should be the walking wounded of the 1980s debt crisis. Rapid industrialization through importing machinery and developing high energy dependence, compounded by the astronomical rise of energy costs in the 1970s, has produced the whopping $800 billion Third World debt. Hardly any country in the export race has failed to incur some sort of debt to subsidize exports. Incurring massive debt to subsidize the integration of its economy into the world economy triggered the Polish crisis that led to the crackdown on Solidarity. A significant portion of the United States indebtedness has been incurred in the subsidization of exports, notably food and arms. The United States is sloughing off its heavy indebtedness to the rest of the world and to the next generation—a privilege accorded only to the number one nation.

The prescription of the market worshippers for dealing with the debt crisis is a large dose of austerity, a word that evokes monkish virtues, but obscures what really happens when countries "tighten their belts." The International Monetary Fund attaches as conditions for new loans and rolling over existing debt the devaluation of currency, abandonment of government welfare and job creation programs, abandonment of price controls, and subsidization of basic needs. In Mexico an estimated one million workers in the construction industry lost their jobs as a result of IMF-mandated austerity. A farmer in poverty-stricken northeast Brazil finds that government credit for essential fertilizer is cut off. Workers in Manila are greeted with a sudden 30 percent jump in bus fares. Industries lay off workers as they are forced to cut back on imported machinery and industrial inputs. In 1983, according to Richard Feinberg of the Overseas Development Council, $50 billion flowed out of developing countries to service debts owed to private banks and multilateral lending institutions against which only $35 billion in new loans flowed in. Despite the success of a few authoritarian Asian countries—Singapore, Taiwan, South Korea—in integrating themselves into the world economy on comparatively favorable terms, for most of the world the term "developing country" is becoming more and more of a euphemism.

The most developed nation in the world is now administering some of the same austerity medicine to itself and is showing some of the same symptoms of de-development—loss of jobs, decline in health, nutrition, and public transportation, and cutbacks in welfare programs for the poor but not the rich. In some of the census tracts of the capital of the world's richest nation the infant mortality statistics resemble the pattern of poor countries, and in Detroit, just to take one obvious casualty of deindustrialization, the rate is rising alarmingly.

The crisis of the world economy defies any easy ideological solutions. There is no system waiting in the wings to be tried. But an alternative future must be invented. For this to happen, the world economic crisis must be seen for what it is, a security crisis that dwarfs all others, one that cannot be addressed by any nation alone but only by the cooperative efforts across ideological and geographical lines, across stages of development, of a community of nations with the imagination to see that global solutions and local solutions must be pursued together.

What, for example, can be done about the worldwide problem of work? First, we must recognize that its dimension and character is different from what we have experienced before. United States workers are now part of a global labor market which is radically affecting their job security and wages. Because of the growing disconnectedness between American-based firms and the national territory, merely increasing the investment capital of such firms will not necessarily create jobs in the United States. It is neither wise nor practical to force companies to produce in the United States when it is uneconomical to do so. But there are many aspects of United States law, such as tariffs, taxes, and permissive labor and environmental standards abroad, that act as powerful incentives to accelerate the loss of jobs with a decent wage. These incentives should be examined carefully and changed.

There should be a public commitment to the idea that every inhabitant must have an opportunity to make a productive contribution to society and to develop as a full person. The words we use so casually to set the very premises of our society—"opportunity" and "productivity"—must be rethought in the light of the real world we face. The idea that members of the society, even a majority of the society, should base their prosperity on the exclusion of fellow citizens from the chance to contribute to their society is morally unacceptable and economically wasteful. It is now commonly asserted that 7 percent unemployment or more is "necessary" to prevent inflation. This newly conventional wisdom is attractive to some because it provides a permanent downward drag on wages. This wisdom, I believe, is false. But if by any chance it should turn out to be true, the society should recognize the heroic contribution of the unemployed to economic stability and reward them handsomely for keeping the economy afloat. I suspect that in those circumstances our attitudes toward the acceptability of other people's unemployment might change.

Work could be more equitably shared. The share of profits going to labor as a whole could be negotiated so as to reduce the incentive to lay off individual workers. The employment implications of labor-saving technology could be debated in affected communities before the decisions are taken. The definition of work could be expanded in a number of ways. Computer technology could be used to enrich, rather than fragment and "de-skill" jobs if government policy encouraged it. The federal government could commit itself to creating new markets in socially useful areas such as health, the arts, retraining and education, and public transportation. After all, it creates markets for arms. Human activities essential for a decent and caring society—maintaining contact with the elderly, visiting sick people, child care—should be regarded as socially productive work for which decent wages should be paid. Here too the practical effects of the existing incentive system—welfare laws and the like—should be reexamined. Welfare programs are now fragmented into those addressed to the middle class (Medicare, social security) which, on the whole, work pretty well, and those provided for the poor (Medicaid, public housing) which don't. The invidious differences in treatment for the survivors and the losers should be ended since the humiliations and inefficiencies of many of the antipoverty programs simply perpetuate the social and class divisions in our society.

There are currents in the American character that complicate the solution to the related problems of unemployment and poverty. One is our fascination with lotteries. Riches are like lightning. They can strike anyone. When George McGovern, in what he thought was a populist appeal, suggested during his 1972 presidential campaign that no American should be able to leave more than one million dollars to his children, he infuriated millions of Americans who are statistically certain to die penniless. Why? Because he attacked the rags to riches myth which legitimizes the way we arrange our affairs as a society. It is acceptable that we live with great inequalities, even that the inequalities grow, provided the opportunity to rise above the crowd is preserved for everybody. American individualism assigns personal responsibility for failure. That is why it is so easy for us to abuse the victims of the economy as lazy or welfare cheats. The frontier mentality lingers. There was no safety net on the Oregon trail. But there were strong families and a sense of community that no longer exists in a society in which 60 percent of black children and 15 percent of white children are being born to single parents.

The lottery mentality encourages the speculation industry. More money can be made more quickly by rearranging stock certificates and building financial pyramids than in producing goods or services. Since smaller companies provide more jobs for each million dollars of investment than huge conglomerates, the current love affair with mergers contributes to the job-destroying process. But we are, as Ronald Reagan shrewdly understood in his presidential campaigns, fixed on growth and productivity as the goal of human endeavor. Serving that goal has produced economic miracles. The argument against any of the approaches I have suggested to the employment problem is that we cannot afford it because it will slow growth and undermine productivity. Charity in small amounts may be an obligation of civilization, but to compensate people for "work" for which there is presently no adequate market is to waste capital that could have been invested productively. The trouble with this way of looking at the world is that it avoids the economic, not to mention the human, cost of abandoning people: thirty thousand dollars a year to maintain someone in prison. One hundred thousand dollars of high-tech heroic measures to save a premature infant who for a few dollars of decent prenatal care could have been carried to term. The sharp rise in child abuse and domestic violence in households where there is an unemployed parent has been documented. The unstated and uncalculated cost of "saving money" by cutting education and library budgets is that we are endangering the community by confronting it with large numbers of angry, isolated people who cannot cope. As long as we keep two separate sets of books, one for the firms who can show impressive productivity and profits by sloughing off all social costs onto the public and another for the community which is going deeper and deeper into debt, we will never know whether our austerity programs are saving money or costing money. If the only legitimate basis on which an individual born into our midst or welcomed to our shores becomes a full participating member of the American community is his or her contribution to the economy, then the opportunities to contribute must be expanded in new ways.

Finally, we cannot begin to make progress toward alternative models of development that can work for rather than against the majority of people on the planet until we heed Confucius's wise counsel and start calling things by their right name. When 40 to 50 percent of world trade consists of transactions within the same multinational corporation, it is absurd to talk about the "market" as if it were an old-fashioned bazaar. We cannot continue to ignore what the market actually is in the closing years of the twentieth century, the freedom it brings, the freedom it destroys, the possibilities it offers, and the illusions it encourages. The key to prosperity, the key to preserving and expanding freedom, lies in a deeper understanding of how the incentives operating on our most powerful economic units actually work.

IV B
DALE R. WEIGEL

Richard Barnet's essay raises a host of questions about the nature and character of the current foreign economic policy of the United States. The basic question he raises is one that has been the subject of debate for as long as nations have had commercial relations. Barnet asks: what is the role of the market and what is the role of government in determining our international economic affairs? His answer is not clear-cut, for he calls into question the relevance of all the main ideological models, ranging from central planning through social democracy to free market models that have guided economic policy making over the last hundred years.

One thing is clear from the experience of the last decade. That is that foreign economic policy cannot be separated from domestic economic policy. The exchange rate for the dollar has a dramatic impact on domestic employment and the prospects for export industries like agriculture. Import tariffs, foreign aid, and policies toward multinational enterprises all interact with domestic monetary and fiscal policy to affect the well-being of the domestic economy.

It is almost a cliché to say that the international economy has become more integrated over the last several decades. Goods markets have been integrated by a progressive reduction of barriers to trade, both official and economic. Tariffs have been reduced, as have transport and information costs. A start has been made to tear down the nontariff barriers erected by governments seeking some control over the supply of goods to their national economy. The result has been a greater variety of goods available at lower cost in virtually all countries (except perhaps the command economies of the Soviet bloc). These benefits have not come without costs, however, for increased openness to trade has produced greater uncertainty for individual industries, and the need for more flexibility and adjustment as individual industries are increasingly buffeted by competition.

Accompanying the integration of goods markets has been a more recent integration of international capital markets. The dismantling of exchange controls and the increasing willingness of financial intermediaries and brokers to operate across national boundaries have resulted in the development of a largely unregulated international capital market which can move large quantities of funds among countries. As in the case of the integration of goods markets, the development of international capital markets has increased the availability of capital from commercial sources to projects and countries that earlier would not have had access. Large volumes of capital flows can be mobilized. But these benefits, as in the case of integrated goods markets, come at a cost, and that cost is the greater instability in the availability of capital that always seems to accompany unfettered financial markets.

Finally, integration of the international economy has been promoted by the development and spread of multinational corporations, firms that plan and produce with an international horizon, allocating production and sales in such a way as to take advantage of the lowest costs and the best markets. An increasing number of firms from the industrial countries, and now even from some developing countries, have begun to plan and produce on a multinational scale.

With increasing integration, the ability of nations to maintain an independent foreign economic policy is called into question. It is difficult for a nation, even one as large and powerful as the United States, to set an independent policy course. This fact was clearly demonstrated by the inability of the Mitterand government in France, early in its term, to pursue an expansionary economic policy in the face of deflationary pressures elsewhere. French policy was quickly brought into line by the unsustainable balance of payments deficits. The United States has been more successful in being an "engine of growth" in the international economy, but even that has been contingent on foreign capital inflows which, if not forthcoming, would force a change in policy.

The international economy has become increasingly integrated because more and more scope has been given to market decisions. This has prompted innovation and the efficient use of resources. At the same time, increasing reliance on the market raises a question about the role governments can and should play particularly in the international sphere, where at one time government intervention weighed heavily on transactions. What are the roles of government regulations and government-sponsored institutions in a dynamic international economy that is increasingly open to market forces?

The question, of course, is particularly significant for the two Bretton Woods organizations, the International Monetary Fund and the World Bank, which were created at the end of World War II to help stabilize the international economy and promote economic development. These institutions were created precisely because it was felt that the market had failed in the 1930s, and that such failure led to worldwide economic depression and ultimately to war. But what today is the role of these two institutions in an international economy that is increasingly integrated and increasingly driven by market forces?

Clearly, that role is changing. With a change in its Articles of Agreement in 1978, the IMF is no longer the keeper of a fixed exchange rate system. Yet the fund still acts to provide liquidity to countries that have become overextended and unable to meet their obligations in the integrated and sometimes volatile world economy. The fund also has become an arbiter of economic policy in countries seeking its assistance, and in this role it provides a seal of approval that commercial financial markets rely on in making new lending decisions.

The role of the World Bank is still in transition. The bank, of course, still focuses on promoting the economic development of poor member countries. However, increasingly it tries to do so by encouraging countries to follow policies that will increase the availability and efficient use of resources from the market, both domestic and foreign. It also tries to use its own resources in a way that mobilizes resources from other market sources, such as commercial banks and direct investors.

Both the fund and the bank, then, are in the process of adapting their modes of operation to the developing international market economy. Changes in the operations of the bank and the fund reflect the desire on the part of governments to encourage the efficiency and dynamism of the market while maintaining institutions that can protect against some of the excesses and risks that the market imposes. There is, in fact, a continuing trade-off between the efficiency and dynamism of the market and the stability that can be provided by government actions to regulate and supersede market forces. It is the tension between these two objectives that is the subject of the international economic policy debate.

The choices that governments have made between these alternatives have fluctuated over time. As I noted earlier, in recent years economic planners have given increasing weight to the benefits of the market. This emphasis has not been limited to the industrial countries. Even the developing countries, many of which had earlier emphasized central planning in their economic policy making, have now given greater scope to market decisions. These changes in policy have been made as the costs of government interference in the market have become more evident. These costs are reflected in waste of investment resources, inefficient use of other resources, and a lack of innovation that erodes the capacity of nations to compete in the increasingly dynamic world economy. The changes also have been undertaken as the success of some countries that have followed a market-oriented policy has become evident.

There are, of course, dangers of relying too heavily on the market, both in the international and in the domestic economy. Many of those

dangers are cited in Barnet's essay. He rightly does not distinguish between problems in the domestic and international economy. He mentions the build-up in external debt of developing countries and the resulting increase in interest and principal payments to service the debt;
declining exports and reduction in industrial production and employment in the United States; a shift of low-paying industrial jobs to Third
World countries; an increasing dependence of some countries on exports for economic growth. It is, of course, not clear to what extent these
"problems" are due to excessive reliance on the market or, for that matter, whether they are all in fact problems. Many would argue, for example, that the increasing division of labor and export dependence is a
benefit, not a cost. It is also possible that some of the problems arise
from continued government intervention. Barnet mentions the $140
billion "corporate" welfare payment in the United States, and we might
also note that much of the vast debt in the world economy was accumulated by governments financing government programs, not by commercial borrowers financing projects.

It is also clear, moreover, that an equally lengthy list of "problems"
could be attributed to excessive government intervention in domestic
and international markets. That, of course, is the reason why economic
policy making has increasingly emphasized markets. The list of such
problems would surely include the economic crisis in Africa where in-
terventionist policies in agriculture have led to declining food production, increased imports, and famine—in a continent that not too many
years ago was a net exporter of food crops.

The experience in recent years has shown that while there are large
returns to be had from reliance on the market to mobilize and allocate
resources, there are also high risks. There are dangers of instability in
the availability of commercial funds, for example, to countries that have
come to rely heavily on such sources. Many of the high debt countries
have found that a stable net inflow of funds from these sources cannot
be assured, and when these funds are withdrawn what appeared to be
manageable debt service requirements suddenly become unmanageable.
These countries are then faced with making difficult adjustments in
their economies to service foreign debt.

What then are the alternatives? Should domestic and international
economic policy go back to a heavy reliance on interference with market
forces? Should trade barriers be erected once again to protect steel
workers in western Pennsylvania and auto workers in the Midwest? The
answer is no. International economic policy cannot, and should not, go
back to an earlier era of heavy controls. The costs are too high in terms
of immediate losses of production and opportunities foregone. That
does not mean, however, that there is no scope for regulation and public

policy. Markets do not always function perfectly, and governments may set out to accomplish public purposes that the markets cannot accomplish on their own.

The foreign economic policy of the United States has long reflected an abiding faith in the efficacy of the market in guiding economic decisions. This faith derives from our own experience and can be said to be a part of the American character. Thus, it was the United States that led the postwar effort to tear down trade barriers. The United States has pressed for freedom of international capital flows and, by deregulating domestic financial markets, has provided increasing scope for the integration of world capital markets.

At the same time, other aspects of the American character have tempered the unbridled rule of the market place. One of these is generosity, which is reflected in the willingness of the American people and the government to help others less fortunate. Thus, the United States has been quick to respond to cases of desperate need, such as the current famine in Africa. The United States led in the establishment of the World Bank, and has over the years, through support of the Multilateral Development Banks as well as through bilateral aid, supported economic development in poor countries. Unfortunately, the intensity of United States government support for development programs has slipped markedly, and the United States now gives only one-fourth of one percent of its gross national product in the form of aid to developing countries. By this measure, the United States ranks sixteenth among the seventeen advanced industrial countries that are members of the OECO Development Assistance Committee.

United States economic policy, therefore, has been guided by a mixture of motives, sometimes emphasizing the market and at other times focusing on objectives that can only be achieved by the government's desire to promote the general welfare. At issue is usually the appropriate mixture of these approaches in particular circumstances. In recent years most attention has been given to exploiting the "magic of the market." As some of the shortcomings and risks of that approach become evident, there is no doubt that the direct role of government, operating through institutions and policy, will to some extent be utilized to restore a balance.

CHAPTER V

Ethnicity and Race as Factors in the Formation of United States Foreign Policy

Introduction

A neglected area in the study of foreign policy development is the influence of American ethnic and racial groups. We have come a long way from the days of our founding fathers when the conduct of foreign affairs lay almost exclusively in the hands of a small, elite group. Until the end of World War II, Americans involved in foreign policy came out of the eastern establishment and were generally educated in private schools and universities. They were usually white, male, Anglo-Saxon, and had independent financial means.

Now we have a professionally staffed Department of State which includes a significant, if not in everyone's judgment an adequate, minority representation. In addition, other agencies of government, members of Congress, and special interest groups influence foreign affairs by making recommendations to—or setting limits to—our international policies. However, in spite of the growth of professionalism in policy making, it should be noted that as many as 40 percent of the ambassadors appointed by recent presidents have been men and women whose chief qualification has been their financial contribution to a political party.

Elliott P. Skinner provides a fascinating history of the influence of racial and ethnic minorities who, despite their nearly complete lack of representation in the corridors of power, still had considerable influence upon policy making. He selects some of the major immigrant groups and describes their efforts to affect policy. Because of their sensitivity to issues involving their country of origin, these immigrants could be helpful in evaluating the effect of American policies on their homeland. At other times ethnic groups have been strong partisans for a particular cause within their former homeland, and their influence has been accordingly narrow. The black population of the United States, even though long separated from meaningful contact with its African homeland, is uniquely qualified to understand racial prejudice. Recently the black community has become heavily involved in pressing our country to condemn apartheid policies in South Africa. Whatever the merits of each individual lobbying effort conducted by ethnic groups, the general and salutary effect has been to oblige the United States to take more seriously its relationship with the countries from which these groups emigrated.

ELLIOTT P. SKINNER is well qualified to speak from both scholarship and experience on these matters. He has had a long and distinguished career in teaching, writing, and public service. He received his B.A. from New York University and later a Ph.D. from the department of anthropology at Columbia University in New York. Dr. Skinner has been the recipient of a number of fellowships and research grants including a Guggenheim Fellowship in 1971. He was a fellow of the Woodrow Wilson International Center for Scholars in 1981 and is presently the Franz Boas Professor of Anthropology at Columbia University. He has lectured and written on a variety of social, cultural, and political issues primarily concerning the continent of Africa. He is the author of The Mossi of Upper Volta: The Political Development of a Sudanese People (Stanford University Press, 1964) and African Urban Life: The Transformation of Ougadougou (Princeton University Press, 1964) and is the editor of seven other books. In 1966 he was asked by President Johnson to be United States Ambassador to Upper Volta, where he served until 1969.

V
ELLIOTT P. SKINNER

THEORETICAL AND PRACTICAL CONSIDERATIONS

Ethnicity and race have played a more salutary role in the formation of United States foreign policy than is usually admitted. Normally accused of harming the national interests by their advocacy on behalf of ancestral ties, America's ethnic and racial minorities often oblige the foreign policy making establishment to examine its own biases, thereby better serving the interests of all Americans.

Given the nature of the ethnic and racial mélange that went into forming the United States of America, a number of the founding fathers—including Madison and Washington—were deeply concerned that factionalism might hurt the emerging nation. In the *Federalist Paper* Number 10, Madison warned against combinations of citizens who, "united and actuated by some common impulse of passion or of interest," may be adverse to the rights of other citizens, or to "the permanent and aggregated interests of the community."[1]

Intimately involved as he had been in the divisive Gênet Affair in 1793 and with the Alien and Sedition Act of 1798, George Washington cautioned in his farewell address that the primary allegiance of all Americans should be to the nation. He urged: "Citizens by birth or choice of a common country, that country has a right to concentrate your affections. The name of America which belongs to you in your national capacity, must always exalt the just pride of patriotism more than any appellation derived from local discriminations."[2] Washington primarily feared those "local discriminations" that came from ethnic concentrations within the United States. He felt that it was only in "union" that Americans

> would experience that "security from external danger, a less frequent interruption of their peace by foreign nations, and what is of inestimable value, they must derive from union an exemption from those broils and wars between themselves which so frequently afflict neighboring countries."[3]

Except for the division between North and South over the question of race and slavery during the Civil War, it was increasing ethnicity that created the "local discriminations" that eventually did affect the United

States and trouble those responsible for its foreign relations. This was perhaps inevitable given the changing demographic profile of the nation. Initially a society of "Englishmen" whose values permeated the emerging nation, the United States soon became a "nation of immigrants." Whereas between 1861 and 1870, 87.7 percent of the immigrants came from northwestern Europe, by the turn of the century a concentrated wave of some 70.8 percent of all immigrants were coming from southeastern Europe. Moreover, this flood came at a time when America was emerging as a world power, when liberal revolutionary movements were affecting Europe, and when racial theories asserting the superiority of Anglo-Saxon peoples were abroad in the land.

A concern for preserving American values and for maintaining a homogeneous American culture revived the antiforeign feelings of the Know-Nothing movement of the 1850s. In reaction, the Congress passed an immigration law in 1924 with a "national origin" quota designed to favor white, Anglo-Saxon, and northern European immigrants. But this action came too late to change the demography of the country and its ethnic complexity. By 1976, the bicentennial year, nearly fifty million representatives of almost all nations of the world had settled in the United States.[4]

Glazer and Moynihan believe that "without too much exaggeration it could be stated that the immigration process is the single most important determinant of American foreign policy."[5] They admit that United States foreign policy "responds to other things as well, but probably *first of all* to the primal facts of ethnicity."[6] Over the years many scholars and statesmen not only have noted the ethnic factor in our foreign policy but also have railed against it. Theodore Roosevelt was particularly hostile to the attempts of ethnic groups (often then referred to as "the hyphenates") to influence American foreign policy. In a speech in 1895 he inveighed against the particularisms of "the hyphenated Americans—the German-American, the Irish-American, or the Native-American." He warned that unless all of these groups considered themselves "American, pure and simple" then the future of the nation would be impaired. Woodrow Wilson attributed the propensity of many American ethnic groups to seek the interests of their ancestral lands to the fact that "only part of them has come over" from the old countries.[7]

Ethnicity was viewed as an important factor in American foreign policy in the years prior to, during, and after World War II. When the United States entered World War II, the editors of the influential *Fortune* magazine warned that "There is dynamite on our shores." They felt that while some immigrant European groups unqualifiedly supported the war, others somewhat reluctantly supported it, while still others submitted to the war effort with traces of subversive defiance. The editors wondered aloud whether the United States could transform this mélange into a "working model of political warfare."[8] There was apparently less question of the potential disloyalty of Japanese-Americans; they were systematically rounded up and incarcerated in concentration camps.

Polish-Americans exerted a great deal of pressure on President Roosevelt during his negotiations with the Soviet Union on the projected postwar boundaries between the USSR and Poland. They felt that the settlement at Yalta made a mockery of the Atlantic Charter and urged congressmen and senators not to ratify the agreement. When President Eisenhower came to office, many citizens of Central European origin wanted the United States to "liberate" their ancestral lands. Even though these groups generally failed in their effort "to force the government to do something it did not want to do, on occasion they have been able to sabotage steps that Washington would have liked to undertake."[9] George F. Kennan, America's brilliant ambassador to the Soviet Union, remarked bitterly in his *Memoirs* that Croatian-Americans "never failed to oppose any move to better American-Yugoslav relations or to take advantage of any opportunity to make trouble between the two countries."[10]

Jimmy Carter, whose presidency witnessed enormous pressures from America's ethnic groups attempting to influence his foreign policy, complained in his farewell address: "We are increasingly drawn to single-issue groups and special-interest organizations to ensure that whatever else happens, our own personal views and our own private interests are protected. This is a disturbing factor in American political life."[11]

Another recent attack on the efforts of minorities in the United States to influence our foreign policy came from Senator Charles Mathias, Jr., of Maryland. Putting the matter bluntly, he declared that "ethnic politics, carried as they often have been to excess, have proven harmful to the nation."[12] Mathias updated George Washington's concern that factionalism—in this case, ethnicity—can generate both unnecessary animosities among Americans and create among them illusions of common interests with outsiders where in fact none exist. He expressed alarm at the attempts by American ethnic groups to put pressure on both the domestic and foreign policy making institutions of the United States to adopt measures in favor of their lands of origin. This included Afro-Americans lobbying on behalf of Africa, Caribbean peoples on behalf of the people of the Caribbean basin, Greeks lobbying both the president and Congress against granting arms to our NATO ally Turkey, Jewish groups promoting the cause of Israel, Mexican-Americans and Italian-Americans supporting immigration policies to benefit Mexico and Italy, and Polish-Americans and some Central and northeastern Europeans attempting to enlist the aid of the United States against Soviet activities and presence in their ancestral homes. Mathias did not suggest that the ethnic advocacy of Americans was unpatriotic. He did stress, however, that the administration's "resistance to the pressures of a particular group in itself signals neither a sellout nor even a lack of sympathy with a foreign country or case, but rather a sincere conviction about the national interest of the United States."[13]

Senator Mathias's concern that ethnic advocacy on behalf of specific ancestral lands may not be in the national interest should be examined theoretically as well as practically: what, in fact, is the national interest? Historically, the answer for American democracy has been: the national interest is what the public—or the electorate—wants. As Charles Evan Hughes once remarked: "Public opinion in a democracy wields the scepter.[14] In his famous debate with Senator Douglas, Abraham Lincoln declared: "With public sentiment on its side, everything succeeds; with public sentiment against it, nothing succeeds."[15] The problem, of course, is that public opinion is often awkward to describe, elusive to define, difficult to measure, and impossible to see, even though it may be felt. A far greater conundrum for the citizens of the United States is that while equality is a basic political tenet, true equality has always been undermined by the reality of socio-economic ranking and stratification within the society. There have always been groups of Americans who have believed they have a better sense of what is in the national interest than their fellow citizens. Moreover, these groups assume, even if they do not claim it publicly, that their view of what the national interests are should be accepted because they have a greater stake in the society than do other Americans.

Senator Mathias is right that such assumptions of inequality have no legitimate place in American society. But it was not too long ago that American citizens who differed ethnically and racially from the majority were viewed as being only partly American, and the assumption was that as a result they should be excluded from the debate over what was in America's national interests. Agreeing with Woodrow Wilson for one of the few times in his life, Theodore Roosevelt said of ethnic Americans: "When two flags are hoisted on the same pole, one is always hoisted undermost. The hyphenated American always hoists the American flag undermost."[16]

The dilemma of relegating ethnically and racially different Americans to the bottom rungs of American society and then accusing them of not knowing what is in the national interest has not escaped the notice of some political theorists. Bailey, in explaining how the "man in the street" reacts to our foreign policy, stated bluntly that the United States has "traditionally been a Protestant and a north European country." This fact has always influenced how immigrants were seen and how they were permitted to participate in our society. Bailey warned that there "is ideally no place in the American pattern for citizens of inferior rank, but if we insist on creating them by our snobbery and prejudice, we must share the blame if they [i.e., ethnics] resist the processes of Americanization." Nevertheless, Bailey felt strongly that ethnics should not hold views about the national interest that differ substantially from those of the dominant American groups. He lamented that the "existence of a great foreign fungus has beyond any doubt seriously hampered the formulation and execution of a rational and national foreign policy." The danger, for him, was that the existence of hyphenates "consistently placed us at the mercy of events abroad; foreign convulsions became our convulsions."[17]

The often hidden assumption that ethnically and racially different Americans are inferior to the dominant groups in defining and protecting America's national interests is usually linked to two other questionable assumptions: that America's dominant groups are not swayed by biases when they define our country's national interests; and that because of their position and "objectivity" they are best qualified to make and execute a foreign policy designed to protect those interests. The fact is that dominant American groups, like human beings everywhere, also have their "irrational" biases. Moreover, these groups do not always include the "brightest and the best" persons to conduct American foreign policy. Roger Morris, who worked daily in the presence of President Nixon, Chief of Staff Alexander Haig, and Secretary of State Henry Kissinger, declared:

> There is no documentary evidence—save perhaps the inaccessible White House tapes on national security subjects—that . . . racism was the decisive influence in Kissinger-Nixon policies in Africa, Vietnam, or elsewhere, policies for which there were other arguments and reasons, however questionable. But it is impossible to pretend that the cast of mind that harbors such casual bigotry did not have some effect on American foreign policy toward the overwhelming majority of the world which is nonwhite.[18]

The underlying presupposition, simply put, is that "from the beginning the United States had an identifiable set of principles and values that were inherited from our English forebears and that their principles and values were superior to all others."[19] Theodore Roosevelt, who was associated with America's rise to the status of a world power, firmly believed in the "white man's burden," in the superiority of Europeans, especially of the Anglo-Saxon, and considered both imperialism and colonialism inevitable. In his book *Winning the West* (1896), he rationalized the liquidation of the Native-Americans on the grounds that they, like the "backward" peoples of Africa, China, India, and the Philippines, were doomed. Roosevelt believed that "The most righteous of all wars is a war with savages, though it is apt to be also the most terrible and inhuman." But he felt also that "the rude, fierce settler who drives the savage from the land lays all civilized mankind under debt to him, American and Indian, Boer and Zulu, Cossack and Tartar, New Zealander and Maori—in each case the victor, horrible though many of his deeds are, has laid deep the foundations for the future greatness of a mighty people."[20]

So "natural" do the biases of the dominant American groups appear that people do not often recognize their role in forming United States foreign policy and in determining what is in the national interest. For example, it has been remarked that the American Aid-to-Britain movement during the early stages of World War II was initiated, not because Germany posed a threat to the United States, but "simply because the vast masses of the dominant old-line American strain reacted instantly and passionately to England's sudden and extreme danger—England: the home of Magna Carta, of Shakespeare and of Milton and Keats and Shelley, of the King James version of the Bible; their imperishable home." The "special" relationship of "old" Americans to England was no more clearly expressed than when in February 1914, in presenting the newly appointed American ambassador to the Court of St. James to the New Hampshire legislature, Governor Robert O. Blood, an old-stock Yankee, called the envoy "the man who is going over to represent us in our fatherland." Some seven members of the legislature, either conscious of their alien background, of the uproar caused by the activities of the German-Americans, or simply because they were "American-firsters," protested that "England was not 'our fatherland,'" that "we Americans cannot have two fatherlands."[21] But the governor offered no correction. He probably considered his detractors to be not only "boors" but "anti-American" to boot.

The assumption that a small number of persons from among America's elite are best capable of formulating and executing United States foreign policy is only now being scrutinized and questioned. Roger Morris called attention to the danger posed to the United States by having its foreign policy under the control of "a small, ingrown elite of men clustered in New York and Washington." He tells us that these men "awaited the call from the White House to determine America's role in the world, or to judge the fitness of one of their colleagues who would. The call usually came."[22] Schooled in selected private academies and colleges and later employed in prestigious old law firms, major banks, corporations, and foundations, these persons, usually white males, have generally been considered to be among the best and the brightest. Yet their position in the American social hierarchy frequently made them oblivious to or contemptuous of the views of other Americans and of most of the country. They were also largely contemptuous of Congress and believed that the general American public knew, or needed to know, little about foreign policy.

The assumptions that dominant American groups have a better judgment as to what is in the national interest than subordinate groups and that a small elite is better qualified than others to formulate and to execute United States foreign policy is a danger to the country—especially in periods of rapid change. One important reason is that many members of this establishment seldom recognized the role of institutionalized and habitual interactions—and often unarticulated ideologies—in the making of foreign policy. Moreover, they are also often unaware of the established patterns of nondisclosure and noninteraction which support largely unconscious and unarticulated patterns of interaction, customs, and manners.

What the ethnic and racial groups can accomplish in attempting to influence United States foreign policy decisions is to subject the foreign policy making process itself to scrutiny and to raise questions about whether certain decisions are really in the national interest. By challenging certain premises of our foreign policy, ethnics raise our level of consciousness and often force the establishment to articulate the basis of its judgment. When challenged, it is surprising how often those responsible for our foreign policy claim "privileged information," "gut-feelings," and "superior experience" as rationalizations for being unable to explain their positions. Because of their ambiguous position as subordinates within American society, but also being members of it, ethnics often see the implications of United States foreign policy in ways that the established practitioners do not. Thus simply by raising questions about American foreign policy ethnics force a reexamination of it. And while ethnics often raise questions related to the interests of their lands of origin, there is no reason to suppose that the discussions those questions stimulate do not rebound to the best interest of the United States. After all, these groups are sometimes better informed about conditions in their lands of origin than the majority of Americans.

Gabriel A. Almond once argued that the attempts of ethnic and linguistic groups to influence American foreign policy have historically been "mainly directed toward traditional national aims such as the preservation or return of national territory, the achievement of national independence, or the protection of minority ethnic or religious groups in foreign countries from persecution by the dominant groups."[23] Thus one has to consider whether the attempted role of American minorities

to raise questions about United States foreign policy is really a threat to
our national interest or is only a threat to those persons and groups who
resent any challenge to their definition of what the national interests
ought to be.

IRISH-AMERICANS AND UNITED STATES POLICY
TOWARD THE "IRISH" PROBLEM

Today the Irish have been so assimilated into American life that no less
than twelve of them have served as president of the United States.
Therefore, it is surprising to hear contemporary discussion about
whether earlier generations of Irish Catholics played a salutary or a negative role in the formulation of United States foreign policy. The Irish
first came to British North America in small numbers, frequently as in-
dentured servants and transported criminals. But after the 1840s, Irish
immigration swelled to more than two hundred thousand poor, sometimes destitute people fleeing famine and starvation in their home coun-
ties. The newcomers were rejected and discriminated against by the An-
glo-Americans in the large northeastern cities where they primarily
settled. They were the objects of riots, job discrimination, and religious
bigotry and were accused of being responsible for creating the first
slums in American cities. Nevertheless, forming voluntary associations
as a means of adapting to urban life and participating in and eventually
controlling the political system in many cities, numerous Irish gained
middle-class status. They adopted many American values and are now
largely conservative in outlook. But so persistent was religious bigotry
against the Irish-Americans, that when John Kennedy ran for president,
he was obliged explicitly to assure American Protestant leaders that, if
elected, he would not be controlled by the Pope in Rome.

Whether it was their ancient history of oppression and persecution,
or the discrimination and the economic competition they found in
American cities, the Irish nurtured an Anglophobia which quickly led
them to seek to influence their new country's foreign policy against
Great Britain. The Fenian Brotherhood, a secret, oath-bound society
organized in New York City on St. Patrick's Day, 1858, committed
members of the American Irish community to the forcible overthrow of
British power in Ireland. The Fenians swore to use any and all American institutions to accomplish this act. Taking advantage of federal
anger at the Confederate use of Canada as a sanctuary for attacking
Union targets, the Fenians invaded that country in May 1866 as a way
of getting at the British. President Andrew Jackson tolerated this act for
domestic political reasons, and Secretary of State William Seward appreciated its foreign policy leverage against Great Britain. However,

when the Fenians attacked Canada again in May 1870, the United States Marshall for Vermont arrested their leaders, because the United States was at peace with Great Britain.

Although many Americans criticized the Fenians, their raids against Canada did convince British Prime Minister William Gladstone and the London Foreign Office that the "Irish" question had "an American dimension." No longer could the British treat Ireland with impunity. This fact was underscored again when, during the Irish land war of 1880–81, prominent members of Congress, spurred by their Irish constituents, pressured the White House and the State Department to seek the release of Irishmen, including some Irish-Americans, who were incarcerated without right of trial by jury. This pressure worked, and London capitulated on the condition that the individual Irish-American agitators leave Ireland and promise never to return. But when in 1888 Sir Lionel Sackville-West, the British ambassador to Washington, suggested in a letter that British interests in Ireland were safe with Cleveland in office, the reaction of an aroused Irish-American community led the president to ask for the ambassador's recall.[24]

Much to the annoyance of Secretary of State John Hays and Theodore Roosevelt, Irish-Americans agitated for the United States to denounce Britain's role in the Boer War. Here was a case in which there was worldwide sympathy for the Boers who were seen as victims of British capitalist imperialism. Nevertheless, Hays was allegedly so passionately pro-British that he could not understand friendliness for the Boers except in terms of partisanship of some sort. He was therefore convinced that Americans who were neutral or pro-Boer had to be Irish or German haters of England, or Democrats trying to embarrass a Republican administration. The feisty Roosevelt, for his part, had a certain sympathy for the resistance of the Boers, but as he wrote in 1899, they were "battling on the wrong side in the fight for civilization and will have to go under." Roosevelt's bias was clearly seen when he declared that the position of the English-speaking people in the world would be greatly weakened and there would be "race humiliation" of a catastrophic sort if the Boers should score a victory in the Transvaal.[25] Both Roosevelt and Hays were outraged when the Clan na Gael's veteran Fenian leader, John Devoy, welcomed Boer envoys to the United States, and actually sent fifty or so Irish-American volunteers to fight against the British in South Africa in the guise of a Red Cross contingent. Irish-Americans were convinced that American national interests were incompatible with close Anglo-American relations. They protested vigorously, and while their actions may not have been the determining factor in our policy, the fact remains that the so-called "Roosevelt-Lodge-Hays group" maintained rigid technical neutrality while hoping that Britain would win in the Boer War.

Some have suggested that second generation Irish-Americans who committed themselves to help liberate Ireland did so in order to overcome their social and psychological inferiority within the United States. Whether or not that was part of their motivation, they did in fact provide "refuge for Irish rebels, economic support for their endeavors, press support for their cause, and political pressure on the State Department, White House, and Congress to support British settlement of the Irish question."[26] Initially siding with German-Americans against United States support of Britain during the opening years of World War I, Irish-Americans nevertheless rallied around the flag when this country entered the war on the side of the Allies.

But Irish-Americans continued to raise the legitimate question whether the continued conflict in Ireland did not impede Britain's war effort. Seeking to drive home this point, Irish-Americans put pressure on 134 members of the House of Representatives to cable the British prime minister urging settlement of the Irish question.[27]

As soon as World War I ended, the Irish-Americans again increased their pressure on the United States to help free their homeland. When the Sinn Fein won a smashing victory in the general election in December 1918, they demanded that at the Versailles peace conference, Wilson should strive to apply the principle of "national self-determination" to Ireland.[28] The British government's refusal to permit a delegation from Ireland to attend the Versailles conference so angered Irish-Americans that at a race conference meeting held in Philadelphia in February 1919, they chose three of their own delegates to go to Paris. Lloyd George, the British prime minister, succeeded in denying the Irish-Americans a hearing at the conference, but "he did permit them to visit Ireland to inspect conditions for themselves on the mistaken assumption that President Wilson wanted him to do this."[29]

Unfortunately, Warren G. Harding (who benefited from the defection of Irish-Americans from the Democratic party) was no more in favor of an Irish republic than was Woodrow Wilson. He expressed his regret to the British ambassador for the strain that the Irish problem had created on Anglo-American relations.[30] Irish-American pressure did, however, force Harding to reprimand Admiral Sims for remarks in which he criticized his fellow citizens for asserting their constitutional rights. Apparently currying favor from a British audience, Sims said of the Irish:

> They are like zebras, either black horses with white stripes, or white horses with black stripes. But we know they are not horses—they are asses, but each of these asses has a vote, and there are lots of them. One inconvenience of a republic is that these jackass votes must be catered to.[31]

The Senate, however, reacted to Irish-American interests and overwhelmingly passed a resolution urging Irish home rule. The British government signed an Anglo-Irish Treaty on December 6, 1921, and many Irish-Americans regarded this treaty as a vindication of their long and bitter struggle to free at least part of their land of origin.[32]

With the growth of isolationism following World War I, Irish-Americans had little success persuading Congress not to pass restrictive immigration laws in 1921 and 1924 limiting the number of potential Irish immigrants. Nor did they seek to use United States influence to stop the fratricidal struggle in Ireland. Whether they feared events in Ireland would fuel anti-Irish sentiment in the United States, or simply because the Great Depression forced them to concentrate on life in the United States is still a subject for debate. Irish-Americans made little effort to influence the United States to remain neutral during World War II, nor did they criticize American objections to Irish Prime Minister de Valera's declaration of neutrality. Obviously Irish-Americans agreed with their fellow countrymen that de Valera's action was against America's national interests.

Initially Irish-Americans felt that there was little that the United States could do when Northern Ireland became a battleground between the IRA, the Catholics, the Protestants, and the British government. But when Ulster appeared to be on the verge of civil war in the late 1960s, Irish-Americans again began to take notice and to look to the United States to do something. Deeply shocked by the events of "Bloody Sunday," January 30, 1972, when British paratroopers killed fourteen Catholic demonstrators in Londonderry, Senator Edward Kennedy of Massachusetts led the Irish-American community in condemning the British use of force. Testifying before a congressional committee on foreign relations, Kennedy declared: "Fifty thousand Americans died before we learned that tragic lesson in Vietnam, and there can be no excuse for Britain to have to learn that lesson now in Ulster."[33] He introduced a resolution in the United States Senate calling for the withdrawal of British troops from Northern Ireland and the establishment of a united Irish Republic. Invoking the ethnic factor, the senator declared, "Ireland has given much to America, and we owe her much in return."[34]

The problem for Senator Kennedy and for the other members of the so-called Irish-American "Four Horsemen" (including Senator Daniel Patrick Moynihan, former New York Governor Hugh Carey, and Speaker of the House Thomas O'Neill) is that although they wield a great deal of power within government agencies, the issue of Ulster poses foreign policy questions difficult for the United States to handle. In contrast to the clear case of British imperialism in southern Ireland, Ulster's dilemma involves the issue of "civil rights" for both Catholics and Protestants, IRA terrorism (said to be linked to Libyan sponsored international terrorism), fears of Marxist influence, and basic Anglo-American relations. Whereas in 1971 Senator Kennedy could demand that Britain immediately withdraw from Northern Ireland and that those Protestants who rejected the notion of a united Ireland "should be given a decent opportunity to go back to Britain," by 1973 he had to acknowledge that "Ulster is an international issue."[35] Moreover, disagreement within the Irish-American community about the best course of action prevented any consensus about what United States foreign policy should be. Despite a joint appeal issued on St. Patrick's Day in 1977 condemning the IRA as the real obstacle to peace in Northern Ireland, the choice of a supporter of the IRA to be the grand marshal of the St. Patrick's Day parade produced anger and a boycott of the celebration by members of the "Four Horsemen."

Deciding that internal division within the Irish-American community was hurting the cause of the Catholics in Northern Ireland, the "Four Horsemen" did use their political clout to approach the United States administration for help. They obtained the support of Secretary of State Cyrus Vance for a plan to provide $100 million in American aid to help toward a solution for Ulster. President Carter also promised to encourage substantial American investment in Northern Ireland provided the British could effect a settlement between the contending parties there.[36] As if to underscore the British government's continued recognition of the Irish-American factor in Anglo-American relations, Prime Minister Margaret Thatcher gave the *New York Times*—but not a single British newspaper—an exclusive interview about her proposal for devolving political power in Northern Ireland a week before publicly announcing the plan.[37]

GERMAN-AMERICANS AND UNITED STATES POLICY TOWARD GERMANY

In contrast to the Irish-Americans with whom they collaborated in an effort to influence United States foreign policy against Great Britain, German-Americans have had very little impact on the foreign affairs of the United States vis-à-vis their ancestral land. This is all the more remarkable since they have historically represented the largest non-English-speaking group of immigrants in the country and have traditionally played significant roles in our history. Descended from the tens of thousands of so-called Palatinate Boers who settled in the mid-Atlantic states and the more than seven million immigrants who arrived in this country between 1820 and 1977 (settling primarily in the Midwest), the Germans were said by some historians to be the one group which desired to colonize the United States. German associations flourished, and persons of German origin became famous statesmen, scholars, soldiers, industrialists, and artists. But like other immigrant groups, the Germans aroused the sort of xenophobia demonstrated in the Know-Nothing movement. And while many Americans appreciated the German choirs, orchestras and beer-gardens, they were wary of the political refugees known as the "forty-eighters," who were regarded as freethinkers, socialists, anarchists, and radicals. Nevertheless, the Germans prospered, voted in large numbers, and played an important political role in the domestic politics of the areas in which they settled or to which they increasingly diffused.

What created a foreign policy dilemma for both the German-Americans and the architects of United States foreign policy was the pride which many German-Americans felt in the aggressiveness of the new nation of Germany which was unified under Prussian control. Initially, the American community at large seemed more amused than irritated by the immense display of Teutonic energies. But the suggestion, in some German-American quarters, that Wisconsin might qualify as a distinct German state was not well received; nor was German-American approval of the Kaiser's saber rattling, especially when this involved American interests in the Samoan Islands.[38]

German-Americans applauded, but were suspicious of, the decision of the United States to remain neutral during the early days of World War I. Many believed that this policy was really traditional American Anglophilia at work, covertly designed to aid the Allies.[39] Very much aware of the mounting agitation among German- and Irish-Americans about the conflict, President Wilson reiterated: "We definitely have to be neutral since otherwise our mixed populations would wage war on each other." But when it became clear to German-Americans that "neutrality as the President practiced it meant American acquiescence in British control of the seas and the outpouring of munitions and war supplies from the United States to the Allied countries,"[40] they reacted strongly. They felt, and perhaps with some justification, that neutrality meant their doing everything possible to prevent Britain from getting an undue advantage in the effort to obtain American arms. In fact, Secretary of State William J. Bryan acknowledged to Walter H. Page, our ambassador to Britain, that the German-Americans had a point, since the United States allowed the "sale of contraband" knowing full well that the Germans could not take advantage of the opportunity to buy.[41]

Not only did the German-American associations attack United States policy but also prominent individual German-Americans joined the fray. In November 1914 a noted Harvard professor warned Wilson about a "political upheaval" among German-Americans. He declared that they had made a firm decision to turn away from "an administration to which it would otherwise be bound by many ties."[42] Wilson was advised to reread George Washington's farewell address and its warning about "European broils," and German-Americans sarcastically labeled the president, "the servant of John Bull." Concerned about this uproar, Wilson forwarded the Harvard professor's letter to Acting Secretary of State Robert Lansing suggesting, "perhaps it would be wise to take very serious notice of it." In response, the State Department denounced the professor and others like him for attempting to "separate American citizens of German nativity or descent from the general body of the American people" and for arousing the "spirit of racial allegiance" of a body of Americans into showing special favors to Germany and Austria despite America's policy of neutrality.[43]

What especially alarmed American foreign policy makers were German diplomatic attempts to use German-Americans for propaganda purposes. In January 1916, James W. Gerard, the United States ambassador in Berlin, reported that the German foreign minister, protesting American arms sales to the Allies, had warned that if the extent of the sales became known to the American people, there was the possibility of "500,000 trained Germans in America" joining the Irish to start a revolution to upset the Wilson administration. The ambassador wrote Wilson that at first he thought that the foreign minister "was joking, but he was actually serious." The next month Ambassador Gerard also reported that he had received word from Henry Morgenthau, Sr., United States ambassador to Turkey, that the German foreign minister had inquired "if it was not true that German-Americans in the United States would rise to rebellion should trouble occur between Germany and America."[44]

Confronted with the specter of German-Americans making foreign policy an issue in the presidential campaign of 1916, President Wilson was advised to ask the Democratic party's committee on resolutions to attack the ethnic blocs by emphasizing "Americanism." The committee drew up a plank in the platform calling upon those "of whatever origin or creed who would count themselves Americans, to join in making clear to all the world the unity and consequent power of America." The platform condemned as subversive

> the activities and designs of every group or organization, political or otherwise, that has for its object the advancement of the interests of a foreign power, whether such object is promoted by intimidating the government, a political party, or representatives of the people, or which is calculated and tends to divide our people.[45]

Politics being what it is, the Republicans were silent on what the Democrats had considered nearly subversive pronouncements by German-Americans and their allies. Responding to what they considered slander by the Democrats, the German-Americans defended themselves by charging that they did not wish to "Germanize" America, but to "deBriticize" it—in order to "Americanize" it. What neither the Republicans nor the German-Americans counted on was Theodore Roosevelt's long opposition to "hyphenates"—or was it perhaps his Anglophilia? Ignoring any damage he might have done to the Republican party, the Rough Rider declared: "No good American, whatever his ancestry or creed can have any feeling except scorn and detestation for those professional German-Americans who seek to make the American President in effect a viceroy of the German Emperor." Accusing German-American leaders of a readiness to "sacrifice the interest of the United States whenever its interest conflicted that of Germany," Roosevelt burdened them with the crime of "moral treason to the Republic."[46]

Germany's unrestricted submarine campaign, coming hard upon the sinking of the *Lusitania* and the attendant loss of American lives, led the United States to declare war on Germany. This was "a tragic hour for German-Americans," but few of them actually protested. One captain in the United States Army, whose father was born in Germany, attempted to resign his commission. He was court-martialed, convicted, and sentenced to twenty-five years in Fort Leavenworth.[47]

The vast majority of German-Americans rallied to the American cause and fought heroically, in spite of the violent reaction of Americans to all things German. Even "sauerkraut" became known as "Liberty Cabbage." But many German-Americans did not forgive Wilson for America's entrance into the war. They were convinced that Wilson's policy, influenced in large part by the traditional "special relationship" between the United States and Britain, had prejudiced their country against their ancestral homeland. They were also convinced initially that the war was not in our national interest. Many German-Americans subsequently opposed America's acquiescence to the harsh terms of the Versailles Treaty and were later among the major supporters of the doctrine of "isolationism" that swept the country between the two world wars.

The rise of Nazism in Germany divided the German-American community. A number of them joined the German-American Bund, but others, like the Steuben Society of America, attempted to straddle the fence. That society pledged "loyalty to the Flag and Constitution of America and its President, and here and now hail both Germany's peerless leader [Adolf Hitler], and America's great President [Franklin Delano Roosevelt]." It noted that while the reaction of Americans to "certain features" of Hitlerism were subjecting American-German relations to "severe strain," it wished to promote "friendly relations between the United States and the country of our forebears, Germany."

What the leaders of the Steuben Society were referring to, of course, was news of Hitler's persecution of the Jews. Some Jewish-Americans were urging the president to do something to help their coreligionists—even to impose a trade boycott. The secretary of the Steuben Society, John Tjarks, wrote President Roosevelt that the "propagation of a trade boycott" was "detrimental to the interests of the American people." He insisted that even the German Jews in "whose interest the boycott is proclaimed" had themselves repeatedly appealed to the world to refrain from actions unfriendly to Germany because those actions only inflamed "already highly wrought feelings." Tjarks also attempted to use America's fear of Bolshevism to defend Hitler. He told Roosevelt that when in 1919 "thousands were killed in the German Civil War against Bolshevism," no country felt constrained to intervene. In conclusion, Tjarks said that his society denied the right of those opposed to Germany "to carry on a high pressure propaganda in this country for the purpose of stampeding it into actions which are contrary to the public welfare, and a menace to its peaceful relations between two friendly nations."[48]

There is no evidence that German-American pressure influenced, in any way, President Roosevelt's attitude toward the plight of the German Jews. Nevertheless, scholars should not ignore the possibility that German-Americans contributed to the total climate in which United States policy failed to help those who later became victims of the holocaust.

German-Americans, however, did not hesitate to join the battle to defend the country's national interest when the United States finally declared war on Nazi Germany. As one historian noted, their behavior was "almost beyond reproach," and they did much to "vindicate our faith in the melting pot."[49]

CENTRAL AND SOUTHERN EUROPEAN ETHNICS AND UNITED STATES FOREIGN POLICY

The twin issues of self-determination and the rise of international communism led groups of central and southern European descent to attempt to influence American foreign policy on behalf of their ancestral lands. More than either the Irish or the Germans, immigrants from these two regions were held in particular disdain. Woodrow Wilson, then a historian at Princeton University writing about these immigrants in his book *A History of the American People* (1903), declared:

... now there came multitudes of men of the lowest class from the south of Italy and men of the meaner sort out of Hungary and Poland, men out of the ranks where there was neither skill nor energy nor any initiative of quick intelligence; and they came in numbers which increased from year to year, as if the countries of the south of Europe were disburdening themselves of the more sordid and hapless elements of their population, the men whose standards of life and of work were such as American workmen had never dreamed of hitherto.[50]

The future president of the United States added that the Chinese immigrants, who had been such a source of controversy in the country, "were more to be desired, as workmen if not as citizens, than most of the coarse crew that came crowding in every year at the eastern ports."[51] When later political opponents of Wilson discovered this statement, the aspiring presidential candidate informed his publishers that he wished to consider rewriting certain passages "in order to remove the false impressions which they seemed to have made." Significantly, after Wilson's reelection in 1916, a new edition of his history appeared—and the passage under attack remained unchanged.[52]

Despite more than their share of the slander, abuse, and traditional prejudices meted out to most immigrants to the United States, the central and southern Europeans organized themselves in their "Little Bohemias," "Little Italies," and "Little Polands" and began to adapt to American life and politics. And like other immigrants before and after, they felt it their right and duty to try to influence the foreign policy of their adopted country on behalf of their lands of origin. Ironically, it was their great detractor, Woodrow Wilson, whom they sought to influence.

The Bolshevik revolution in czarist Russia, coinciding as it did with America's entrance into the war, created unforeseen and potentially difficult choices for United States foreign policy. During the Brest-Litovsk meeting in March 1918, Lenin promised a new deal for European nationalities. Woodrow Wilson, without the knowledge of the State Department, elaborated a policy of "Fourteen Points" which held out the hope of "self-determination" for the downtrodden peoples of the embattled Austro-Hungarian and Turkish empires. Wilson felt that "self-determination is not a mere phrase. It is an imperative principle of action which statesmen will henceforth ignore at their peril." He hoped it would attract central and southern Europeans to the Allied side and that, while spelling disaster for Germany, it would promise a new international order.[53]

Ethnic Americans of central and southern European origins reacted favorably to Wilson's policy, but Secretary of State Robert Lansing had reservations about it. He foresaw a danger that the policy of self-determination would stir up nationalist discontent only to refuse to accept "the extreme logic of this discontent." Nevertheless, he conceded that the policy "would have a very great influence upon a large body of our population." Lansing announced to a meeting of the Congress of Oppressed Races of Austria-Hungary, held in Rome, that the United States took an interest in and had great sympathy for the "nationalistic aspirations of the Czecho-Slovaks and Jugo-Slavs." He also instructed Ambassador Thomas N. Page to explain "confidentially and orally" to the Italian government that United States policy "would result in benefit both to the Czecho-Slovaks and Jugo-Slavs in the United States on their support of the United States in this war; would encourage and greatly increase enlistments in this country for the Czecho-Slovak Legion now acting in Italy with the Italian Army; and would encourage the Czecho-Slovaks and Jugo-Slavs in Austria in their efforts to hamper the Austrian military operations against Italy."[54] Thus the Wilson administration was not averse to using the American hyphenates in the furtherance of the United States national interest.

Encouraged by both the president and by the State Department, Czech, Polish, and Slovak organizations in the United States redoubled their efforts on behalf of their ancestral lands. True, "the American public was not only uninterested in the fate of the Czechs and Slovaks but, with rare exceptions, completely unaware of their existence."[55] Nevertheless, when Thomas G. Masaryk, a Czech nationalist, arrived in the United States, he was well received. Czech-American Adolph J. Sabath introduced him to congressional circles, and on Sabath's behalf Senator William H. King sponsored resolutions advocating an independent "Bohemian-Slovak State." For his part Masaryk "lobbied vigorously in behalf of independence of his people, strengthened the interest of Czech-Americans in their native land, and successfully cultivated important government officials."[56] Those Czech-Americans who met Masaryk in Pittsburg promised to help him in his subsequent meeting with the president on behalf of a Czechoslovakian state.

Unfortunately for President Wilson, not all Americans of central and southern European background agreed with the recommendation of the Versailles Treaty and with his plans for the League of Nations. During hearings on the conference on foreign relations, spokesmen for Slovak, Czech, Estonian, Latvian, Lithuanian, Greek, Hungarian, Irish, and Yugoslav (Slovene, Serb, and Croat) organizations presented claims and counterclaims. Millions of Americans of these ethnic backgrounds realized that the promises and pledges made to them during the war were neglected, refused, or compromised at the conference table. Italian-Americans were especially distressed that the port of Fiume, which they had wanted for Italy, had been given to Yugoslavia. Italian-

Americans continued to denounce the Treaty of Versailles and the League of Nations and helped to defeat the Democratic party in the 1920 election.

Although by the 1930s many Italian-Americans were entering the American mainstream, the group as a whole was not wholly immune to the blandishments of Il Duce on behalf of his fascist regime. Mussolini sent his friend Count Ignazio Thaon di Revel, the nephew of an Italian admiral, to head the Fascist League of America. Many Italian-Americans applauded Italy's defeat of Ethiopia feeling that this victory would raise their status in America. They were therefore disa6ppointed when the United States remained neutral and declined to welcome the conquest of Ethiopia. The Federation of Italian American Democratic Organizations of the State of New York warned President Roosevelt about "the necessity for the United States' recognition of Italy's annexation of Ethiopia in order to secure for the party the entire Italian-American vote [in 1940]."[57]

When on June 10, 1940, during a speech in Charlottesville, Virginia, the president referred to the Italian attack on France as a "stab in the back," Italian-Americans were mortified. One woman asked the president to understand that while Italian-Americans were loyal to the flag and would fight to defend our shores from any invader, she could not understand what they should do when the "English and French" Americans insult Italians. She complained that because the United States was a "divided nation," Italian-Americans were insulted because of their names. This, she asserted, was in contrast to Europe, where "regardless on what side one lives the government is united and all the people are one by birth. In the United States," she concluded, "all the people are citizens and the division only comes according to what side the President takes, for to the ignorant this gives strength to insult the other nationalities."[58] She therefore begged Roosevelt to be careful in his broadcasts. The president replied that he regretted that any public statement of his had "wounded the sensibilities of any loyal citizen or alien." Nevertheless, he said he would continue to criticize fascism.

Italian-Americans, like their fellow citizens, supported United States foreign policy when this nation went to war against Mussolini. But they were not happy with their status within the Democratic party. Many of them were therefore lukewarm to Harry Truman, who had been vice-president under "stab in the back" Roosevelt. As president, Truman sought to win the friendship of Italian-Americans by playing the anticommunist card. The Democrats saturated the Italian-American communities with leaflets recounting how the president had "saved Italy from communism." This apparently led many Italian-Americans to give Truman their vote. He not only welcomed this personal approval but also took advantage of it to further his foreign policy in Italy. Seeking to preserve that country as a major theatre in America's struggle against the Soviets, the White House, the Department of State, and many American leaders urged Italian-Americans to write their friends and relatives in Italy, beseeching them to vote against the Communists. A number of Italian-American pensioners living in Italy were fearful that participating in the Italian elections might jeopardize their citizenship status. They were assured that they could vote against the Communists and remain loyal and respected American citizens.[59]

The outbreak of World War II was viewed as a great tragedy for Polish-Americans. More than most citizens of central European background, they had benefited from Wilson's "Fourteen Points." After some 120 years, Poland was independent, and for this they were grateful. Now their ancestral land was invaded by both the Nazis and the Soviet Union. In the face of initial United States neutrality, there was little that Polish-Americans could do except to support refugees and the "Free Polish" resisters.

When the United States entered the war, the Polish-American Congress attempted to influence Roosevelt's perspective on the Polish issue. The organization even threatened to withhold the vote of Polish-Americans from the Democrats if its advice was not followed.[60] The indications are that Roosevelt had his own agenda. He allegedly did tell Stalin about the views of Polish-Americans when negotiating at Yalta, but the Soviet leader was not impressed. And since the atomic bomb was still not operational, the American president, believing that he needed Russian cooperation in the final thrust against Japan, did not press the point. When the war was over, Polish-Americans were among the first to protest the Yalta agreement. They publicly accused the Allies of sanctioning the postwar domination of Western Europe by the Soviet Union.[61]

The ensuing Cold War posed a problem for Polish-Americans seeking to influence United States policy toward Poland. They wanted United States support for Poland, but they detested the Communist government installed there. Seeking Polish-American support during the 1952 presidential campaign, both American political parties voiced opposition to Yalta and expressed the desirability of freeing "the Captive Nationals" of Eastern Europe. The Republicans consulted with Arthur Bliss Lane, a former United States ambassador to Poland and a person in touch with recent emigrés and exiles in the United States. Lane suggested that Polish-Americans wanted the Republicans to repudiate the Yalta agreement—as well as the Tehran and Potsdam agreements. This, he believed, would gain the support of all disaffected Americans whose homelands had been "sold down the river" by the

Democrats. When the State Department took a weak stand when Polish workers rioted at Poznan in June 1952, Lane complained bitterly. He was even more critical of the Polish-Americans. In a letter to the editor of the *New York Times,* he accused them of being "too lenient in appraising American foreign policy, reminding them that America has reason to thank Poles such as Kosciuszko and Pulaski for contributions to American independence."[62] Adding to Lane's disappointment, the Republican party decided that it was not yet prepared to deal with the ghosts of Yalta and the effect of that treaty on Eastern Europe.

Neither Polish-Americans nor other Americans of Eastern European origin could persuade the Eisenhower administration to intervene when Soviet troops crushed the Hungarian revolution in 1956. The United States felt that it could not deal with Eastern Europe and with the Suez crisis at the same time. The State Department was also caught in a dilemma when Wladyslaw Gomulka, the Communist chief of Poland, electrified the world by withstanding the pressure by a visiting Nikita Krushchev to adhere more closely to Soviet policy. Gomulka heightened the tension by almost immediately seeking economic aid from the United States. The Department of State was prepared to consider his request, but feared that aid to a Polish Communist government might "have adverse political consequences in the United States among voters who demand the complete end of Communist rule in Poland." The diplomats were especially fearful of the reaction of Thomas S. Gordon, the chairman of the foreign affairs committee, a congressman of Polish origin who strongly opposed United States relations with Poland. These fears proved unjustified when, almost overnight, the bravery of Gomulka captured the admiration of most Polish-Americans. They threw their organized force behind the Communist government of Poland in its attempt to obtain United States aid.

This sudden change in the attitude of Polish-Americans was judged by some observers to be "the most dramatic change in political thinking of the last decade." The White House readily accepted an aid program, since agricultural aid pleased farm state legislators as well as the "Polish community in America, and Catholic sentiment in general—both of which favored helping the distressed Poles despite their Communist government."[63] What is surprising is that the State Department did not realize that most ethnic groups relate to their ancestral societies and not necessarily to the governments that rule there. This lack of understanding continues to plague United States foreign policy.

In contrast to the unanimous approval of aid to Poland in 1957, many American foreign policy experts faulted the Congress in July 1959 for adopting unanimously a resolution calling upon the president to proclaim an annual "Captive Nations Week." Senator Charles Mathias specifically charged that this act was not in the best interest of the United States. He complained that the resolution was adopted with little debate or deliberation and that it was "a routine response to the wishes of Americans whose countries of origin had fallen under Soviet domination."[64] The fallout came when, during Vice-President Nixon's visit to the Soviet Union, Premier Krushchev accused the United States of blatant interference in the internal affairs of his country. What Krushchev noted—a fact ignored by many congressmen—was that included among the "captive nations" were independent Communist states as well as such integral units of the Soviet Union as Armenia, Byelorussia, Georgia, and the Ukraine. Vice-President Nixon reportedly

> felt obliged to explain and, in effect, apologize for Congress's action, telling Kruschchev that actions of this type cannot, as far as their timing is concerned, be controlled even by the President, because when Congress moves, that is its prerogative. Neither the President nor I would have deliberately chosen to have a resolution of this type passed just before we were to visit the U.S.S.R.[65]

Mathias concluded that in this case Eastern European Americans acted in a manner detrimental to American foreign policy, especially since issues of great moment were at stake. But granting there could have been better coordination between the White House, the Congress, and the State Department, should Americans abandon the right of petition when they feel aggrieved?

Poland is still an active arena in the Cold War, and continues to preoccupy the United States government and persons of Polish descent. The rise of the Solidarity Movement, the emergence of prominent Americans of Polish descent as members of the foreign policy establishment, and the elevation of a Polish cardinal to the papacy have all tended to increase the interest of Polish-Americans in the foreign policy making process. When President Carter adopted a "hawkish" position vis-à-vis the Soviet Union for invading Afghanistan, Polish-Americans felt that their ancestral land would benefit. The Polish-American Congress encouraged and applauded Carter's promise of $670 million in food credits in 1980 to help Poland out of its deepening economic crisis. In the 1980 election, Polish-Americans gave Carter a majority of their votes, and when he lost, a delegation of Polish-American leaders visited President Reagan in the White House in July 1981. There they reiterated their concern about United States policy toward Poland. They asked the president to back Solidarity and the Polish church, to liberalize the immigration laws as they affected Polish refugees, and to grant federal appointments to deserving Polish-Americans.

It is too soon to tell how Polish-Americans will react to the new attempts at détente between the United States and the Soviet Union. Polish-Americans are more suspicious of the USSR than most Americans and support a stern United States military stance in the world vis-à-vis the Soviet Union.[66]

Due in part to the relations between the United States and the Soviets in the Cold War, Greek-Americans have also attempted to influence American foreign policy on behalf of the people of southern Europe. It was the Truman doctrine of March 12, 1947, that awakened them to the United States's determination to exercise "the primary responsibility, previously held by Great Britain, for the strategic support of Greece and Turkey as barriers to the expansion of Soviet influence in the Mediterranean."[67] Until then, Greek-Americans were only quietly concerned to help their families on both sides of a bitter civil war between Communist and non-Communist forces after the liberation of Greece. They made their voices heard loudly, though, when in early 1956 Great Britain imprisoned Archbishop Makarios of Cyprus for agitating for independence. Members of the American Hellenic Educational Progressive Association and other Greek organizations petitioned the White House, the Congress, and the State Department for help in the release of the archbishop and in gaining self-determination for Cyprus.[68] Makarios was finally freed, and so was Cyprus. But ignoring the fears of the Turkish minority on the island, some members of the majority Greek population sought unity, or *enosis*, with Greece. In July 1974 an enosis-inspired coup (supported by the mainland) overthrew Makarios, creating panic among the Turkish Cypriots over their future. Alarmed by the plight of the Cypriot Turks, Turkey invaded the island and occupied 40 percent of northern Cyprus, where many of the Turks fled. During the conflict, tales of genocidal attacks on the part of both Greeks and Turks shocked the world.

The conflict between two of its allies guarding the southern flank of NATO was judged a disaster by the United States. The State Department wanted to mediate a settlement, but Greek-Americans alarmed over the plight of the Greek Cypriots fastened on Turkey's illegal (that is, non-NATO related) use of United States military supplies. They initiated a debate in Congress about imposing an arms embargo against Turkey. Much to the distress of the State Department and the White House, Congress put the embargo into effect in February 1975. The press exacerbated the issue by charging that the Greek lobby forced many legislators to yield to "pressure." Greek-Americans were said to have been "emotional," "abusive," "relentless," and "even more Greek than the Greek government itself."[69] Many in Congress later admitted that they were made to feel that "a voting bloc is a better friend on election day than a record of commitment to controversial national interests."[70] One congressman allegedly remarked: "Maybe I wouldn't have lost my seat over this, but who wants the hassle?"[71]

Turkey's reaction to the arms embargo was also viewed by the administration as an unmitigated disaster when that government voted to close twenty-six United States bases and listening posts in its territory. Concerned about possible harm to the NATO alliance, both President Ford and Secretary of State Kissinger lobbied Congress in October 1975 partially to lift the arms embargo against Turkey. The administration's fear was not groundless, because the Turks had increased their contact with the Soviet Union. When the prime minister of Turkey returned from a visit to Moscow in 1978 he commented that "the embargo certainly affects our thinking in many ways and encourages us to be more imaginative regarding solutions to our economic problems and to our defense problems."[72] In response, the Carter administration sought to lift the entire embargo, calling it "the most immediate and urgent foreign policy decision" before the Congress. The administration's supporters noted that

> the embargo, after three and a half years, had failed to spur a large-scale withdrawal of Turkish forces from Cyprus or bring the Turks to the negotiating table, while having the undesired effects of alienating Turkey from the United States, impairing our armed forces, denying the United States intelligence on missile tests and troop movements in the Soviet Union, and thus seriously weakening the southern flank of NATO.[73]

Faced with pressure from the Greek lobby, President Carter had to take strong action. Representative Paul Findley of Illinois was quoted as telling him that he needed to do more than "make a few phone calls and have some Congressmen over to the White House for breakfast," because "the opposition is dedicated and strong, and it's been gearing up for this fight for a long time." Senator Mathias reported that in his own remarks in the Senate he felt constrained to state that his position was in no way "anti-Greek," but was based on what he perceived as "American as well as Greek or Turkish interests." Moreover, he attacked the "hyphenates" directly when he quoted Plato to the effect: "There can be no affinity nearer than our own country."[74]

The critics of the ethnic factor in United States foreign policy see the Turkish arms embargo as a prime example of how parochial and particular interests jeopardize United States national interests. The question remains, however, whether Greek-American pressure on behalf of the Greek Cypriots was detrimental to the national interests. Moreover, save for the attention directed to the issue by Greek-American lobbying, it is possible that the Turkish army would have liquidated the Greek Cypriot population. Greek-Americans still remember (though many Americans never knew) what happened to Greeks under unfettered Turkish rule and still blanch at the fate of the Armenians in Turkey. Until the Jewish holocaust, the Armenian massacre was one of the worst instances of genocide in history. Even Senator Mathias recognized this factor in the Greek-American action, when he admitted that "but for the activities of Greek-Americans we might have overlooked, for strategic reasons, the injustices suffered by the Greek population of Cyprus."[75]

THE MISPERCEPTION OF JEWISH-AMERICAN IMPACT ON UNITED STATES FOREIGN POLICY

Jewish-Americans are said to be the ethnic group most involved in attempting to influence United States foreign policy on behalf of their co-religionists around the world. Most other American ethnic groups cite the "Jewish model" when they consider attempting to influence United States policies toward their ancestral lands. And indeed, a number of Jewish and Israeli lobbies are proud of their record in dealing with the Congress, the State Department, and the White House on behalf of world Jewry.

Most Americans readily concede that the centuries-long history of Jewish travail lies at the basis of the Jews' will to protect themselves or, in simpler terms, just to survive. Fear may indeed be the sentiment which leads Jews to ask of any event: "Is it good for the Jews?" The earliest Jews in British North America were rejected by the Dutch in New York, and that treatment reasserted itself later in other parts of the country. Jews had to bear not only the opprobrium shown to many immigrants but also the assiduous anti-Semitism that had been the lot of Jews in Europe for centuries. To make matters worse, incidents involving Jews in other parts of the world eventually disturbed the "domestic tranquility" of Jews even here in the United States.

Partly because of the international repercussions of anti-Semitism, Jewish-Americans attempted to help foreign Jews as soon as they were able to do so. Although then having little political clout, Jewish-Americans welcomed President Van Buren's decision to have the American representative in Turkey intercede on behalf of the besieged Jewish community there. In 1857, Jewish-Americans protested, but were helpless to prevent Millard Fillmore from concluding a commercial treaty with Switzerland, where Jews had been expelled from many cantons. Nor could Jewish-Americans persuade James Buchanan to rescind that treaty with Switzerland, or to have his Secretary of State, Lewis Cass, protest the persecution of Jews in Palestine.[76]

Theodore Roosevelt was not only sympathetic to the domestic aspirations of Jewish-Americans, but he also paid attention to their foreign policy concerns. He instructed Oscar Straus (later to become the first Jewish cabinet member), his representative to the International Arbitration Court at the Hague, to protest to Nicholas II about a pogrom in Kishenev. The czar refused to consider the United States's interference in Russian domestic affairs, but a precedent had been set. Roosevelt's successor, William Howard Taft, was not very helpful to Jewish-Americans. He reneged on a promise he had made to Jewish-American voters to rescind an eighty-year-old treaty with Russia which contained an anti-Semitic clause. The resulting split in the American Jewish community during the 1912 elections harmed the Republicans. Henry Morgenthau's support of Woodrow Wilson, the successful Democrat candidate, gave the Jewish-American community unparalleled access to the White House and leverage on United States foreign policy.[77]

American Jews did not escape the rise in ethnic consciousness characteristic of so many ethnic Americans during World War I. However, for them the "hyphenate" problem was compounded because they had originated in so many lands. Jacob H. Schiff allegedly said: "I am divided into three parts: I am an American, I am a German, and I am a Jew."[78] Other Jews despaired that their allegiance to the United States might conflict with their search for a Jewish homeland. The confusion was compounded by the fact that while many former Russian Jews detested the czar and desired his defeat, those Jews still in Russia supported their country. Russian Jews fought against Kaiser's Germany, a country held in high regard by the German-American Jewish elite. In 1915 the Federation of American Zionists called attention to the dilemma in which Zionists as "citizens of every embattled state . . . [were] fighting with the utmost courage and loyalty in every army," even for those states which were "false to their own solemn obligation" toward other Jewish soldiers.[79]

A combination of factors enabled and stimulated the American Jewish community to attempt to influence United States foreign policy on behalf of the Jewish world: Turkey's entrance into the war on the side of Germany, thereby jeopardizing the Jews of Palestine; British imperial concerns in Europe and the Middle East and their attempt to use Zionism as a propaganda ploy; and the friendship between President Wilson and two important Jewish American leaders, Justice Louis D. Brandeis and Henry Morgenthau, Sr., the United States ambassador to Turkey. Jewish-Americans were also stimulated by a special State Department memorandum, instigated by Louis Brandeis, describing United States help to foreign Jews. Although viewed as a ploy to gain votes for the Democrats in the Jewish community, this report was indeed true. More than once Secretary of State Lansing had instructed a somewhat reluctant Ambassador Henry Morgenthau, Sr., to put pressure on Turkey to ameliorate its policy toward Palestinian Jews. Because of his German-Jewish origin, Morgenthau was sensitive about leaning on the Turks. The irony was that Wilson had sent him to Constantinople with the injunction: "Remember that anything you can do to improve the lot of your coreligionists is an act that will reflect credit upon America, and you may count on the full power of the Administration to back you up."[80]

Because of their strategic positions within the United States foreign policy establishment, Louis Brandeis and Felix Frankfurter were able to work closely with Wilson on the issue of a Jewish homeland in Palestine. The diplomats in the State Department were aware that many anti-Zionist Jews did not favor the homeland policy. But Wilson and his Jewish-American advisors did, and the president gave his support to the text of the Balfour Declaration. He also announced the decision on August 31, 1918, in time for the presidential election. The president's letter to Rabbi Wise endorsing the declaration led Justice Brandeis to remark that "opposition to Zionism could henceforth be considered disloyalty to the United States."[81] And when Henry Cabot Lodge introduced a Senate resolution on April 12, 1922, supporting a Jewish homeland in Palestine, Jewish-Americans felt that they had scored a victory for world Jewry.

The failure of Jewish-Americans to persuade the United States to enunciate a tough policy toward Hitler's Germany early in his rise to power was due primarily to the decision of the Roosevelt administration not to interfere too strongly in the affairs of Nazi Germany. Roosevelt's Department of State refused to permit Jews to bypass restrictive, yet underutilized, immigration quotas, and the president remained indifferent to the plight of Jewish refugees who arrived in the United States without visas. Roosevelt allegedly not only failed to reverse, but in fact encouraged Breckenridge Long's obstruction of attempts to rescue Jews. Described as a "consummate politician," Roosevelt knew that any determined efforts on behalf of the imperiled Jews would reap few tangible rewards among Jewish voters—who had nowhere else to go. While reportedly not unfriendly toward the Jews, he felt any act on their behalf would create a great many difficulties both at home and abroad. He was therefore "simply unwilling to go out of his way to help them."[82]

The so-called *zitterdick* ("don't rock the boat") syndrome among many German-American Jewish leaders (already noted in Henry Morgenthau, Sr., but strong also in the Ochs-Sulzberger family which published the *New York Times*) made matters worse. Many German-American Jews refused to believe the news from Germany. Walter Lippman, the prominent journalist, had such a blind spot for Germany (unless he simply hesitated to betray his fears to other Americans) that he praised Hitler in 1933 as "the authentic voice of a civilized people" and remained silent about the holocaust. Matters were made worse by the disagreement within the Jewish-American community about what to do about German-American propaganda in favor of Hitler. One historian concluded that "much of their formidable organization resources were dissipated in internal bickering until it seemed as if Jews were more anxious to tear each other apart than to rescue their co-religionists."[83]

The influence of Jewish-Americans on Truman's decision to support the partition of Palestine and to create a Jewish state there in 1948 is still debated. What no one could deny was that a combination of factors made this act acceptable to the American people: a feeling of guilt and horror over the holocaust; a weakening of British power in the Middle East with a concomitant rise of American power in the world; the spectacle of Soviet power pushing into the Mediterranean; and the 1948 American presidential elections for which Jewish-American votes were sought. It was of great importance that many Jewish-Americans lobbied incessantly for the creation of the state of Israel. Early in 1948 the head of the Democratic National Committee reported to Truman that there were "Zionist Jews in the office every day" complaining of the party's lack of forcefulness regarding Israel.[84]

On the other hand, the sentiment in the State and Defense Departments was that a pro-Zionist policy would not be in America's national interest. The diplomats and the military argued that with such a policy, Truman might help the Soviets in the emerging Cold War. Both Dean Acheson and General George C. Marshall were concerned that domestic politics might lead the president to take a stand detrimental to our foreign relations. Nevertheless, on Yom Kippur 1948 Truman endorsed the creation of the state of Israel—but still hesitated to make the decision public. Pressure from Jewish-American groups increased to such an extent that Truman later wrote: "I found it necessary to give instructions that I did not want to be approached by any more spokesmen from the extreme Zionist cause."[85] American Jewish leaders had to seek the intervention of Eddie Jacobson, a former business partner of the president, to get the president to invite Dr. Chaim Weizman, the first president of Israel, to the White House. Truman would later insist that it was not the pressures from the American Zionists that led him to recognize Israel, but rather the promises and pledges made by his predecessor and by the Congress. He felt that his decision was in the national interest "because it was based on the desire to see promises kept and human misery relieved."[86]

Today many Americans openly express dismay at the incessant attempts of the Jewish-American community to influence United States foreign policy toward Israel and on behalf of Jews in the Soviet Union. The reason for this activism, according to Stephen D. Isaacs, "is that for the first time in American history, American Jews have felt secure enough in their Jewishness and their Americanism to challenge major aspects of this country's foreign policy, with regard both to the Middle East and to the Soviet Union."[87] Convinced that the national interest as perceived by the American establishment in the 1930s, 1940s, and 1950s did not reflect their concerns, but may in fact have been based on assumptions which hurt them, Jewish-Americans are determined to seek a new consensus.

The event that seemed to stimulate many Jewish-Americans to take a bolder and more activist approach to United States foreign policy was the Suez crisis of 1956. Long smarting under British dominance in their country and disturbed by the American decision not to help support their high dam, Egypt threatened to nationalize the Suez Canal. Reacting to their threat Britain, France, and Israel, all of whom shared a common grievance against Nasser, invaded Egypt. Alarmed by the Soviet threat to pour volunteers into Egypt to protect that country, and faced with the threat of atomic warfare, President Eisenhower reluctantly criticized the invasion. He decided to honor the nonaggression rule in the United Nations charter and supported a cease-fire resolution. The president refused to listen to contrary arguments from the Western Europeans and from Israel's supporters in the United States. Many Jewish-American groups felt that, once again, Jewish interests were being sacrificed to expediency, and not necessarily in America's national interest. Two major Jewish organizations, the Washington-based America-Israel Public Affairs Committee and the Conference of Presidents of Major American-Jewish Organizations, decided to monitor and attempt to influence United States foreign policy especially with respect to Israel and to Jews.

Since the 1967 or Six-Day War, these two organizations have spearheaded major campaigns by Jewish-Americans to develop foreign policy positions on subjects involving Israel. These have included the sale of Phantom jets to Israel in 1968, 1970, and 1971; Secretary of State Rogers's peace plan of 1969; the cease-fire agreement of 1970; the military resupply of Israel during the 1973 war; the Sinai agreement of 1975 formalizing the separation of Egyptian and Israeli forces; and the sale of F-16 and AWACS aircraft to Egypt and Saudi Arabia. The successive Johnson, Nixon, Ford, and Carter administrations all faced pressure from Jewish-Americans who often disagreed with United States policy toward Israel.

Nevertheless, whether their detractors believe it or not, Jewish-

American lobbies have consistently proven sensitive to United States national interests. As the AIPAC insists, "unless you can always translate this in terms of what's in America's interest, you're lost. Yours is just a tiny voice."[88] In fact most observers conclude that as far as foreign policy payoffs are concerned, the "domestic pro-Israel activities have been mixed."[89] Even so, a number of officials responsible for formulating or articulating United States foreign policy have been critical of these activities. One issue has been particularly nettlesome.

Both the Carter and Reagan administrations have expressed deep concern about the impact of the Jackson-Vanik Amendment on United States-Soviet relations. This issue still poses a problem since the Soviets have expressed to President Reagan a desire to increase trade with the United States. The background to this Amendment is not in dispute. Faced with the exodus of many of its better-educated citizens, the Soviets imposed a tax of about $1,340 for a permanent exit visa, with an escalating "compensation fee" designed to repay the state for the cost of education given to its most educated emigrants. This was a problem for all potential emigrants, but Soviet Jews stood to suffer most because of their relatively high educational levels. Convinced that here was a clear case of discrimination against Jews who wished to flee communism, the American Jewish community reacted. They petitioned the Congress, and after long, tedious debates and political jockeying, Congress passed the Jackson-Vanik Amendment in 1974, linking "non-discriminatory trade" with "freedom to emigrate" from the Soviet Union and its clients.

The Soviets were so angered and embarrassed by the bill that they cancelled the 1972 Soviet-American trade agreement and stopped payment on World War II lend-lease debts. Jewish emigration, which had reached a peak of thirty-five thousand in 1973, was reduced to twenty-one thousand in 1974, the year the Jackson-Vanik was adopted, and dropped to thirteen thousand in 1975.[90] This development allegedly so angered Secretary of State Henry Kissinger that, in a meeting with Jewish leaders on June 15, 1975, he declared: "No country could allow its domestic regulations to be dictated as we were pushing the Soviets to do. . . . I think it was a serious mistake that the Jewish community got hung up on it."[91] In retrospect, even some Jewish-American leaders have admitted that the Jackson-Vanik Amendment may have been counterproductive. Hyman Bookbinder of the American Jewish Committee felt that, "Logic told us we might lose the gamble, and it seems like we lost it. What we hoped we could get out of the Jackson amendment did not come to pass." One must admit, however, that Bookbinder does not speak for the hard-line Jewish-American lobbyists.

Senator Mathias considers the Jackson-Vanik Amendment another example of a "product of ethnic politics" which influenced United States foreign policy. He is disturbed that this policy, like others, "remains on the books, [despite] failure on its own terms, and inadvertency in its larger consequences."[92] One may agree or disagree with the senator's assessment. But if, like many Jewish-Americans, one is concerned about the now universal issue of human rights and the need for the United States to support the implications of this issue, then one might not jump to the conclusion that the amendment has been a failure. In an article in the January 29, 1985, *Christian Science Monitor,* Carl Fell noted some of the unexpected effects the pressure was having on the Soviets:

> What might be called the "star wars" era of Soviet behavior is full of surprises. None is more startling than the quiet discussions Moscow had recently undertaken with American Jewish groups to examine long-standing differences over emigration from the USSR. Add that to other unusual behavior and you get a picture of serious intent to negotiate—not only on arms but on trade and other difficult matters.
>
> Marshall Goldman, deputy director of Harvard's Russian Research Center, who has taken part in the discussions, reports that exploratory talk has focused on an easing of trade restrictions on Soviet goods and on Jewish emigration.[93]

THE AFRO-AMERICAN RACE FACTOR AND UNITED STATES POLICY TOWARD AFRICA

For decades, most Americans have all but ignored the interests of black Americans in the plight of Africa. Those interests recently became more visible when, on Thanksgiving Eve, 1984, a number of prominent black Americans (a congressman, a member of the Commission on Civil Rights, and the leader of a black lobby known as TransAfrica) were arrested for "sitting-in" at the South African embassy in Washington, D.C. They had decided to escalate black protests against South Africa's official policy of apartheid and the Reagan administration's policy of "constructive engagement" toward that country.

The centuries-long interest of blacks in Africa has generally been overlooked by most white Americans. In Thomas Bailey's critique of the ethnic factor in American foreign relations in *Man in the Street,* he declared quite openly:

> No mention has been made of the most numerous hyphenate group of all, the Afro-Americans, who constitute about one-tenth of our population. They are racial hyphenates rather than national hyphenates, for they have since lost any foreign nationality.[94]

Bailey did note that when Mussolini attacked Ethiopia in 1935, some

American blacks reacted; one Hubert Fauntleroy Julian ("Harlem's Black Eagle") went to fight in Ethiopia. But in Bailey's view, Julian "was an outstanding exception." He asserted that as far as the Ethiopian war was concerned, "the sympathies of the American Negroes, in so far as they had any, were with their colored brethren."⁹⁵ Bailey was clearly convinced that blacks could have no possible interest in United States foreign policy. Their interest in the Ethiopian war was based not on the philosophically sophisticated notion of *nationality*, but on the more primordial sentiment of *race*.

Because of the importance of race in American life and thought, we can understand why being a "racial"—in contrast to being an "ethnic"—hyphenate was indeed one of the factors that prevented Afro-Americans from participating fully in American life. Slavery was, of course, the other. In contrast to the white colonists (including even bonded servants) who came to these shores, the ancestors of most black Americans were brought here as chattel slaves—as things. A bloody Civil War freed the slaves, but failed to transform them into persons with full civil rights. After more than a century of protests and strivings, the descendants of the Africans are still struggling to achieve full civil and economic equality with other Americans. It has seemed—and still seems—quixotic to most white Americans (and even to some blacks) that Afro-Americans would seek to help anyone but themselves; for as Bailey rightly observed: "To most Americans, God is Nordic, and the black and yellow do not fit into our color scheme."⁹⁶

Paradoxically, because of the color question, Africa itself has been part of the Afro-American's dilemma. Africa's military and political weakness in the global system permitted its people to be shipped off to become the hewers of wood and the drawers of water for others. In times past, some Afro-Americans would have ignored their "africanity" if they could have done so. Barring that, many sought to elevate Africa's status in the global system, using whatever means were available: the church, the school, missionary, and pan-movements, and—when it was finally open to them—the foreign policy of the United States.

Although white Americans helped to found Liberia (primarily as a way to siphon freed slaves out of America), Afro-Americans were the ones who sought to use American power to protect that nation from European conquest. Generations of black diplomats battled the Department of State, the White House, and the Congress to help Liberia survive. In doing so, they had to face squarely the issue of the hyphenate. John H. Smyth, the United States minister to Liberia from 1878 to 1881, once remarked that,

Race allegiance is compatible with patriotism, with love of the land that gave us birth. . . . Though we are part of this great national whole, we are a distinct and separate part, an alien part racially, and destined to be so by the immutable law of race pride, which is possesed by our white fellow citizens, if not by us. The sentiments, the something stronger than sentiment which makes an English-American proud of his connection with Britain, a French-American proud of his connection with La Belle France, and a German-American fondly attached to the memories of the Fatherland, and all European races of their Aryan descent, has something that partakes of the moral sublime.[97]

Largely because of such views, Smyth attempted to persuade Secretary of State Frederick T. Frelinghuysen to use United States power to protect Liberia's territory. In one revealing telegram, Smyth suggested to the secretary that

> if not incompatible with the relations of a foreign mutual friend of England and Liberia, you will make suggestions favorable to the Negro nation's rights as may tend to a final and speedy settlement of the matter in justice and equity to both nations, should you feel called upon to interpose, and your suggested views be heeded. This, I am advised, is the desire of the [Liberian] President.[98]

Smyth also warned that if Britain gained the territory she was after, the local people would become her vassals, and "the oil and forest possessions will be guarded and protected for the enrichment of England, with little reference to whether the Negro benefitted or not."[99]

American secretaries of state were often apologetic about the amount of time devoted to Liberia. Writing to the American minister in Paris, Secretary of State Evarts explained:

> The volume of Foreign Relations for 1879 devoted to the affairs of Liberia [commands] a much larger space than would seem to be warranted by the relative importance of that country. The reason for this is plain, and grows out of the peculiar relations which this country holds toward Liberia, and which are likely to become of increased importance. It is quite suitable that the great powers should know that the United States publicly recognizes these relations, and is prepared to take every proper step to maintain them. In this view, the publication of this correspondence seems not opportune.[100]

Black Americans were among the first persons to attempt to persuade the United States to condemn the brutal rule of King Leopold in the Belgian Congo. Colonel George Washington Williams (who had served in the Union army in the Civil War) was horrified by what he saw in that country during a visit in 1890. He write the Belgian king stating:

> All the crimes perpetrated in the Congo have been done in *your* name and *you* must answer at the bar of Public sentiment for the misgovernment of a people, whose lives and fortunes were entrusted to you by the August Conference of Berlin, 1884–1885.[101]

Williams wanted an international commission and the Anti-Slavery Society to investigate the charges and beseeched the Belgian government "to cleanse itself from the imputation of the crimes" of Leopold. He sent a report on the Congo atrocities to President Harrison, but never received a response. It was only when Booker T. Washington invoked his friendship with Theodore Roosevelt that black Americans were able to join in a worldwide condemnation of Leopold's rule. Much to their satisfaction, the Belgian state finally took control of the Congo.

When Great Britain demanded control of the Liberian customs in 1908, the Liberians asked black Americans to use their influence with the White House to preserve their independence. The "wizard of Tuskegee" asked President Taft to receive the Liberian envoys at the White House. He agreed and instructed Secretary of State Knox to appoint a commission to Liberia "to investigate conditions there and to report how this country can best serve the republic of Liberia in the present exigency."[102] On the other hand, the lack of a personal Afro-American contact with Wilson (the black vote in the north was not very important) and the president's own bigotry prevented Afro-Americans from vigorously pressing Africa's case at Versailles. The American delegation was especially hostile to Dr. W. E. B. DuBois's efforts on behalf of Africa. Wilson refused to grant him an audience at the peace conference and allegedly tried to have Clemenceau, the French premier, expel him from France. It took the personal intervention of Blaise Diagne, an African deputy from Senegal, to persuade Clemenceau to permit DuBois to convene the 1919 Pan-African Congress.[103]

Except for the Italian-Americans—with whom blacks symbolically fought out the Ethiopian war in the streets of East Harlem—most Americans, like Thomas Bailey, never noted the interest of Afro-Americans in that conflict. But as Roi Ottley wrote:

> From the beginning, the Ethiopian crisis became a fundamental question in Negro life. It was all but impossible for Negro leaders to remain neutral, and the position they took towards the conflict became a fundamental test. The survival of the black nation became the topic of angry debate in poolrooms, barbershops and taverns.[104]

Afro-Americans were terribly frustrated by their inability to mobilize American and world opinion against Italy. Writing in *Foreign Affairs* about the "Inter-Racial Implications of the Ethiopian Crisis," Dr. DuBois voiced the "lost faith" of blacks "in an appeal for justice from the United States in this war or in any affair that concerned black people."[105] Dr. Willis W. Huggins, a Harlem physician, organized petitions to the League of Nations on Ethiopia's behalf, declaring that the Fascist destruction of Ethiopia would imperil world peace. He also attacked the United States and the Soviet Union for remaining neutral in the face of such a gross violation of the League of Nations' Charter. But there is little evidence that United States policy makers even noticed these concerns of black Americans.

Perhaps because Hitler had carried racism to its logical extreme and because blacks had participated with distinction in the war effort, President Truman did appoint a number of blacks as United States delegates to the United Nations inaugural sessions in San Francisco in 1945. One of them, Dr. DuBois, was scandalized by the contradictions he encountered: here was Britain pleading for a world of free states and democracy, while holding millions of colonials in thralldom; Jan Smuts waxing sentimental about "humanity" while pursuing repressive policies against blacks in South Africa; even our own Secretary of State James Byrnes arraigning the Soviets for the absence of democracy in Russia while blacks in Byrnes's own South Carolina could not vote.[106]

It was the success of the postwar nationalist movements that stimulated black Americans to make a determined attempt to influence United States foreign policy. Britain's decision to grant independence to Ghana on March 6, 1957, presented all Americans with a problem: what would be the impact of this development on both American domestic and foreign policies? Many Afro-Americans viewed Ghana's independence as an opportunity to breach that elite structure which made or influenced United States foreign policy. President Eisenhower, who wanted to enlist Africans on America's side in the Cold War, sent Vice-President Nixon to Ghana's independence celebrations. Attempting to reconcile America's domestic attitudes toward Afro-Americans with a forward-looking foreign policy toward Africa, the State Department agonized over whether to appoint a black or white American as ambassador to the new state.[107]

Personal ambition aside, many Afro-Americans saw in a possible Ghanaian ambassadorship an opportunity to establish good relations between Ghana and the United States, and at the same time to advance the status of blacks in America. They believed that sending a black ambassador to Ghana would signal the country's willingness to deal with Afro-Americans in a new way. On the other hand, blacks feared that if Ghana rejected a black ambassador, racists in America could claim that even the Africans did not want Afro-Americans. In fact, a few white journalists reported that Ghana had reservations about recognizing a black ambassador. Few persons understood that both the Ghanaians and the Americans were caught in a bind. The Ghanaians might prefer an ambassador from America's dominant group—a desire consistent with their own pride and national sovereignty. Yet the presence of a white American ambassador would always remind them that he represented a country in which blacks were considered inferior and unworthy to represent their country.[108]

The arrival of the first Ghanaian diplomats in this country did have an impact on the relationship between Afro-Americans and white Americans. When Mr. Gbedemah, the finance minister of Ghana, was refused a glass of orange juice in a restaurant along Route 40 in Maryland, President Eisenhower felt obliged to invite him to the White House for breakfast. This gesture was designed to soothe the feeling of Mr. Gbedemah, but it served to highlight the contradictions between the rhetoric of the champions of world democracy and racist America. It also forced local officials throughout the United States to realize that their domestic race relations were being internationalized to an extent that they had not foreseen.

By the early 1960s, members of the white American foreign policy establishment began to discuss openly the implications of America's domestic posture toward Afro-Americans and its foreign policy, especially toward Africa. To cite an example, Rupert Emerson, writing in *The Centennial Review* (1960) about "American Interest in Africa," stated:

> Speaking in human terms, the greatest of our interest is the fact that a tenth of our population found its distant origin in Africa. Increasingly, as Africa has forged ahead in the world of recent years, American Negroes have watched it and have taken pride in the advance which is being made, as other migrants to the United States have rejoiced in the achievements of their forebearers.... Looked at the other way around, the way in which the United States treats its Negro citizens is of immense importance for the Africans to whom the news penetrates quickly of discrimination and desegregation, of Supreme Court decisions and Little Rock. ... American pledges of good will and good intent are then inevitably measured against the treatment which the Negro receives at home.[109]

Meanwhile, the new African states began to attack American racism and to reject its foreign policy overtures. Jaja Wachuku of Nigeria told the fifteenth General Assembly of the United Nations: "Anybody who is not prepared to eradicate that humiliation that has been meted out to people of African descent or people of our racial stock cannot claim to be in love with us."[110] A few months later, African presidents meeting at the Organization of African Unity in Addis Ababa rejected a goodwill message from John F. Kennedy beamed down from Gordon Cooper's spacecraft. They said in an open letter to the president:

The Negroes who, even while the Conference was in session, have been subjected to the most inhuman treatment, who have been blasted with fire hoses cranked up to such pressure that the water would strip bark off trees, at whom the police have deliberately set snarling dogs, are our kith and kin. . . .The only offenses which these people have committed are that they are black and that they have demanded the right to be free and to hold their heads up as equal citizens of the United States.[111]

By 1962, black leaders working through the American Society for African Culture and the American Negro Leadership Conference on Africa felt that the time had come to mobilize and to articulate the Afro-Americans' heightened interest in Africa. They declared that Afro-Americans should actively attempt to influence United States policy on behalf of Africa as the Jews did on behalf of Israel and the Irish on behalf of Ireland. The ANLC declared:

We rededicate and reaffirm our ethnic bond with and historic concern for the peoples of Africa, and our complete solidarity with their aspirations for freedom, human rights and independence.

We commit ourselves to a wholesome involvement in the affairs of Africa, and the yearning of the African people for full freedom, and we call upon the entire Negro community in the United States to join with us in this commitment to the end that our total influence as a group will be used to aid Africans in their march towards freedom.[112]

Responding to the Afro-American leadership, President Kennedy assured the ANLC that he shared their belief that the twenty million black Americans "had a responsibility for the role of the United States in Africa." The black leaders gladly accepted his words. They took the opportunity to voice their concerns about United States policy in Africa to Secretary of State Rusk, Assistant Secretary for African Affairs G. Mennen Williams, Governor Harriman, and other Kennedy officials who attended their conference in September 1964. This activity continued during the late 1960s and early 1970s. The goal repeatedly expressed was "to politicize the masses of black people to put pressure on black politicians to get them to speak up in America for Africa in the way that Jewish politicians speak up for Israel."[113]

President Nixon's victory over the Democrats in 1968 was viewed as a tragedy for Afro-Americans interested in United States policy towards Africa. In a now infamous Memorandum 139, Henry Kissinger postulated that "wars of national liberation" could not succeed in southern Africa, that only the local whites could ameliorate the plight of blacks there, and that conflict in the region could only aid the Communists. Under the guise of encouraging peaceful change in the region, Nixon's national security chief encouraged Africans to establish a dialogue with South Africa. Yet, when Kenneth Kaunda of Zambia wished to discuss with the president the statesmanlike Lusaka declaration, Nixon could not arrange a meeting. And to the chagrin of Afro-Americans, the United States took other anti-African measures. Congress decided to exempt chrome from the United Nations trade embargo against Rhodesia. Then the administration used its very first veto in the Security Council against a resolution expanding sanctions against the Rhodesian rebel regime.[114]

Afro-Americans reacted as best they could to Nixon's African policy. The African Liberation Day committees organized "marches" on Washington to protest the administration's Rhodesian and South African policies. Students at Southern University picketed the unloading of Rhodesian chrome ore at Baton Rouge, Louisiana, and were supported by the black longshoremen of the International Association. The Afro-American workers of the Polaroid Corporation in Boston linked their struggle with those of the firm's black workers in South Africa. Throughout the country, Afro-Americans and whites joined in urging multinational banks and businesses to curb their relations with South Africa. The congressional black caucus passed several resolutions critical of United States policy in Africa, and the delegates to the National Black Political Convention meeting at Gary, Indiana, on March 10–12, 1972, lamented their relative lack of influence on United States policy toward the "homeland" and vowed to help change it as soon as possible.

The congressional black caucus became particularly alarmed when Secretary of State Kissinger attempted to intervene in the Angolan civil war. They mobilized their allies in a wary Congress and encouraged a war-weary nation to reject Dr. Kissinger's Vietnam-like premise and promise—that a little aid to Holden Roberto of the F.N.L.A. and Jonas Savimbi of U.N.I.T.A. would turn the tide. Secretary Kissinger was convinced that Agostinho Neto's victory in Luanda would resurrect the specter of falling dominos, this time in southern Africa. And when his pleas failed he lamented that "the world watched with amazement, our adversaries with glee, and our friends with growing dismay, how America seems bent on eroding its influence and destroying its achievements in world affairs through an orgy of recriminations."[115] Working closely with other legislators, the black caucus forced Ford and Kissinger to recognize that blacks were a new force in the formulation of policies towards Africa.

On April 14, 1976, for the first time in the history of the republic, a secretary of state found it expedient to discuss American foreign policy issues publicly with Afro-Americans. Meeting with the congressional black caucus, Kissinger discussed his forthcoming African trip. He attempted to persuade the black legislators that his policies held out the best hope for peace in southern Africa. The caucus had been critical of his past attitude towards Africa and now recommended that the United States should: 1) recognize and support the M.P.L.A. in Angola; 2) oppose bantustans (separate black homelands) and support majority rule in southern Africa; 3) repeal the Byrd Amendment which admitted Rhodesia chrome ore to the country; 4) mend relations with Nigeria; and 5) reaffirm United States commitment toward participation in a multibillion dollar aid package for the Sahel region of West Africa.[116]

Black Americans had no faith in Republican policies either at home or in Africa. They were also now quite conscious of the power of the black vote in the coming 1976 presidential elections and were determined to wring pledges from the Democratic candidates for a new African policy. In September 1976, a group known as the Black Leadership Conference on Southern Africa issued "The African-American Manifesto on Southern Africa." It stated, in part:

> There comes a moment in the affairs of humankind when honor requires an unequivocal affirmation of a people's right to freedom with dignity and peace with justice.
> Conscious of our duty to speak, and recognizing our responsibilities to humanity and to the revolutionary ideals of our forebears, we, the descendants of Africa, meeting in Washington, D.C., on this 100th anniversary of the first modern war for independence, proclaim our unswerving commitment to immediate self-determination and majority rule in Southern Africa.
> We do this because we are African-Americans, and because we know that the destiny of Blacks in America and Blacks in Africa is inextricably intertwined, since racism and other forms of oppression respect no territories or boundaries.[117]

The Democratic nominee Jimmy Carter told the Afro-American community that "It would be a great help to this nation if people in public life were to be made aware of the problems of Africa through a significant black interest in Africa." He added that,

> There is no question that Africa has been ignored since the days of John F. Kennedy. Africa should become, and will become, one of the major foreign policy issues of the coming decade. Many of our domestic and international problems will be determined by the direction of our policies in Africa.[118]

Speaking for President Ford and the Republicans during the 1976 campaign, former California governor Ronald Reagan not only criticized past United States policies in Africa but also asserted that, if a Republican administration were asked to send a token force to Rhodesia in order to preserve the peace and to prevent bloodshed during the transfer of control to black majority rule, it should do so. Reagan was speaking less on behalf of President Ford than for the right-wing Republicans who felt that Kissinger had surrendered to communism in selling out the white minority in Rhodesia and that he would ultimately betray South Africa.

Carter's victory in November 1976 held out the promise to Afro-Americans that they would have the opportunity to help the United States formulate its African policy. The president's choice of Andrew Young as his ambassador to the United Nations was an indication to blacks that Carter planned to honor his campaign promises to improve the United States's relations with Africa. Almost immediately the administration successfully effected the repeal of the Byrd Amendment. Then on March 14, 1977, in a speech before the United Nations televised nationwide, President Carter called for black majority rule in southern Africa as the only means of keeping peace there. The president linked his policy toward Africa with his concern for human rights the world over.[119]

Meanwhile, Ambassador Young, with the aid of Great Britain's Foreign Minister David Owen, shuttled between Washington, London, Salisbury, and Pretoria reviving the stalled talks over the future of Zimbabwe-Rhodesia and Namibia. Young was able to gain the support of the front-line African states in southern Africa for the United States initiatives and to win over other African states, especially the increasingly powerful Nigeria. Indeed, for a while, it appeared as though Afro-Americans were in charge of all aspects of United States African policy. When Young was not talking to African presidents, his deputy, Donald McHenry, was negotiating with the South Africans, British, Canadians, and French over Namibia. Both diplomats met substantial success in their endeavors. For the first time in more than a decade, the United States was respected and admired both at the United Nations and in Third World capitals.

Afro-Americans did express alarm when in 1978 the Carter administration, concerned over civil strife in Angola, Namibia, and Zaire, blamed the Soviets and began to retract from Carter's earlier commitment to rapid political change in South Africa. Secretary of State Vance told the Senate Foreign Relations Committee that the United States "understands the difficulties involved in change within South Africa. We are not seeking to impose a simplistic formula for South Africa's future."[120] With this statement, the Carter administration appeared to be moving back to the thesis of Kissinger's Memorandum 139. Its view now was that it was inadvisable to support those forces seeking internal change in South Africa while that country was attempting to find solutions to the problem of Namibia.

Although not entirely happy with Carter's foreign policy toward Africa, black Americans preferred it to what they knew about Ronald Reagan's views about that continent. The Republican nominee in 1980 had spoken out earlier on Zimbabwe, and blacks had no reason to think that his views on Africa had become any more enlightened. Therefore, blacks were not surprised when the newly elected Reagan chose as his Assistant Secretary of State for Africa Chester Crocker, who like Kissinger before him felt that:

> The real choice we will face in southern Africa in the 1980s concerns our readiness to compete with our global adversary in the politics of a changing region whose future depends on those who participate in shaping it.[121]

As far as Crocker was concerned, the whites in South Africa had overwhelming military power to dictate the terms of whatever happened in the region. Again echoing Kissinger, Crocker believed that apartheid could not be dismantled "through a sudden dramatic act"; therefore he recommended that the United States adopt a policy of "constructive engagement" with South Africa in the hope that the whites would be encouraged to ameliorate the conditions of blacks. Crocker was convinced that "impatience with the inadequate pace of change in general is no excuse for indulging in the applications of pinprick pressures and minor wrist-slapping proposals. These may offer us quick, temporary relief, but in South Africa they only underscore our futility."[122]

Much to the chagrin of Crocker and the administration, TransAfrica, the black lobby on Africa, obtained a copy of a memorandum he had prepared for Secretary of State Haig's meeting with South African Foreign Minister Botha. This "scope paper" revealed much about the hidden agenda of "constructive engagement." Crocker indicated that the political relationship between the United States and South Africa had arrived at a historic crossroads, and he felt that "the possibility may exist for a more positive and reciprocal relationship between the two countries based upon shared strategic concerns in southern Africa."[123] This meant that the United States would not only stop criticizing South Africa but also would relax trade and military restrictions and encourage the relaxation of global pressure on South Africa if the regime promised to ameliorate its domestic policies.

The administration's problem was that South Africa grasped at the opportunity to exploit United States concern over the Soviets while pursuing its policy of apartheid. Reagan's diplomats ignored the Afrikaners' attempts to spread the doctrine of apartheid through a worldwide propaganda campaign. As many Afro-American foreign policy experts had predicted and feared, Reagan's policy toward South Africa has not brought about any movement toward majority rule for Namibia; it has not resulted in truly beneficial and constructive relations between South Africa and its neighbors; and it has not led to meaningful dialogue between the white minority and the black majority within South Africa, despite the rioting and deaths which accompanied the Botha regime's attempt to co-opt Coloured and Indian minorities into a racially restricted new constitutional system. The rising protests of black Americans and their white allies did induce the State Department to admit that it was "deeply disturbed and concerned" over the violence in South Africa. It also deplored the detentions of those leaders who opposed the government. Nevertheless, the Reaganites still described the constitution as a "legitimate" if "flawed" reform.

Most black Americans agree with the basic thrust of the 1981 authoritative report of the Study Commission on United States Policy Toward Southern Africa chaired by Franklin A. Thomas, President of the Ford Foundation. The report declared:

> We cannot ignore South Africa. What happens in that country affects the United States. The uniqueness of apartheid attracts world attention. "What sets South Africa apart from other countries that have equally oppressive human rights records," a United States senator said not long ago, "is that its policies are based on race, made 'legal' through legislation, and justified in the name of defending the West from Communism."[124]

The growing confrontation between the Reagan administration and the increasing agitation of black Americans over our foreign policy toward South Africa bodes ill for our national interest. It would be a pity if the United States were to allow its "no-win" policy toward South Africa to damage our global position.

Scholars and policy makers do not agree whether history has an element of inevitability, but without doubt South Africa possesses all or most of the ingredients for violent civil strife, and the United States is becoming more involved with the problem there. My concern is that the parallels are too close and too dangerous to be ignored. If people make history and history is not made for them, then the Reagan administration should be enterprising enough to stop a dangerous process. It should abandon the disastrous policy of constructive engagement and by this dramatic act initiate a policy designed to help bring about a nonracial social system in South Africa that is struggling to be born. Such an action would do more to secure United States economic and security interest in South Africa, and in the world, than in temporizing with a system that is universally condemned and that contains within it the seeds of its own destruction. If the demonstrations before the South African embassy and consulates in this country can help bring these policy changes about, Afro-Americans would have demonstrated that ethnic and racial minorities can make a salutory contribution to United States foreign policy which is truly in the national interest.

NOTES

1. James Madison, *The Federalist Papers*, ed. Henry B. Dawson (New York: Charles Scribner, 1863), 1:56.

2. George Washington, in *Washington's Farewell Address: The View from the Twentieth Century*, ed. Burton I. Kaufman (Chicago: Quadrangle Books, 1969), p. 18.

3. Ibid., p. 19.

4. Louis L. Gerson, "The Influence of Hyphenated Americans on U.S. Diplomacy," in Abdul Azez Said, ed., *Ethnicity and U.S. Foreign Policy* (New York: Praeger, 1981), p. 21.

5. Nathan Glazer and Daniel P. Moynihan, eds., *Ethnicity: Theory and Experience* (Cambridge, Mass.: Harvard University Press, 1975), pp. 23–24.

6. Ibid.

7. Quoted in Thomas A. Bailey, *Man in the Street: The Impact of American Public Opinion on Foreign Policy* (New York: Macmillan, 1948), p. 16.

8. Ibid.

9. Stephen A. Garrett, "East European Ethnic Groups and American Foreign Policy," *Political Science Quarterly*, 93 (1978), 307.

10. George F. Kennan, *Memoirs, 1958–1963* (Boston: Little Brown, 1972), pp. 286–7.

11. *Vital Speeches*, 47 (Feb. 1981), 226–8.

12. Charles McC. Mathias, Jr., "Ethnic Groups and Foreign Policy," *Foreign Affairs*, 59 (1981), 997.

13. Ibid.

14. Bailey, p. 16.

15. Ibid.

16. Ibid., p. 31.

17. Ibid.

18. Roger Morris, *Uncertain Greatness: Henry Kissinger and American Foreign Policy* (New York: Harper & Row, 1977), p. 23.

19. Theodore Roosevelt, *Winning the West* (New York: Putnam, 1896).

20. Howard K. Beale, *Theodore Roosevelt and the Rise of America to World Power* (New York: Collier, 1956), pp. 147ff.

21. Louis Adamic, *Two-Way Passage* (New York: Harper & Row, 1941), pp. 59–61.

22. Morris, p. 23.

23. Gabriel A. Almond, *The American People and Foreign Policy* (New York: Harcourt, Brace & Co., 1950), p. 183.

24. Marjorie R. Fallows, *Irish Americans* (Englewood Cliffs, N.J.: Prentice-Hall, 1979), pp. 122ff.

25. Beale, p. 100.

26. Graham C. Kinloch, "Irish American Politics," in Joseph S. Roucek and Bernard Eisenberg, eds., *American Ethnic Politics* (Westport, Conn.: Greenwood Press, 1982), p. 205.

27. Fallows, p. 122.

28. Thomas E. Hachey, "Irish Republicanism, Yesterday and Today: The Dilemma of Irish Americans," in Winston A. Van Horne and Thomas V. Tennesen, eds., *Ethnicity and War* (Milwaukee: University of Wisconsin System and American Ethnic Studies Coordinating Committee, 1984), p. 156.

29. Bailey, p. 22.

30. Quoted in Hachey, p. 157.

31. Joseph M. Curran, *The Birth of the Irish Free State, 1921–23* (University, Ala.: University of Alabama Press, 1980), p. 9.

32. Ulrick O'Connor, ed., *Irish Liberation* (New York: Grove Press, 1974).

33. *Congressional Record,* 92nd Congress, 1st Session, 1971, pp. 3672–3.

34. *World Press Review,* Nov. 26, 1979, p. 28.

35. *Foreign Policy,* 11 (1973), pp. 168–71.

36. *New Statesman,* May 11, 1979, pp. 678–9.

37. *New Statesman,* Dec. 7, 1979, pp. 888–91.

38. Klaus Wust and Norbert Muchlen, *The Story of German-American Involvement in the Founding and Development of America* (Philadelphia: National Carl Schurz Association, 1976), p. 4.

39. Frank P. Zeidler, "Hysteria in Wartime: Domestic Pressure on Ethnics and Aliens," in Van Horne and Tennesen, eds., pp. 72–3.

40. Arthur S. Link, *Wilson: The Struggle for Neutrality, 1914–1915* (Princeton, N.J.: Princeton University Press, 1960), 5:20ff.

41. Ibid., 161.

42. Ibid., 163.

43. Carl Wittke, *The German Language Press in America* (Lexington, Ky.: University Press of Kentucky, 1957), pp. 245–8.

44. Louis L. Gerson, *The Hyphenate in Recent American Politics and Diplomacy* (Lawrence, Kans.: The University of Kansas Press, 1964), pp. 50–51.

45. Ibid., p. 65.

46. Theodore Roosevelt, "Theodore Roosevelt to the Progressive National Committee, June 22, 1916," in Elting E. Morison, ed., *The Letters of Theodore Roosevelt* (Cambridge, Mass.: Harvard University Press, 1954), 3:1071–2.

47. Zeidler, pp. 75–76.

48. John Tjarks to Franklin D. Roosevelt, October 2, 1933; quoted in Gerson, p. 113.

49. Ibid., p. 19.

50. Woodrow Wilson, *A History of the American People* (New York: Harper & Bros, 1903), 5:212–3.

51. Ibid.

52. Gerson, p. 63.

53. Ibid., p. 79.

54. Ibid., p. 80.

55. Ibid., p. 80.

56. Ibid., p. 123.

57. Ibid., p. 125.

58. Ernest E. Rossi, "Italian-American Relations with Italy in the Cold War," in Humberto Nelli, ed., *The United States and Italy: The First Two Hundred Years* (New York: American-Italian Historical Association, 1977), p. 113.

59. Herbert Feis, *Churchill-Roosevelt-Stalin: The War They Waged and the Peace They Sought* (Princeton, N.J.: Princeton University Press, 1957), p. 522.

60. Donald Pienkos, "Polish-American Ethnicity in the Political Life of the United States," in Roucek and Eisenberg, eds., p. 284.

61. Gerson, p. 218.

62. Harry Schwartz, *New York Times*, Jan. 27, 1952, p. 1.

63. Mathias, p. 984.

64. Ibid., p. 985.

65. Pienkos, p. 290.

66. Mathias, p. 987.

67. Sallie M. Hicks and Theodore A. Couloumbis, "The Greek Lobby: Illusion or Reality?" in Said, ed., p. 75.

68. Ibid., p. 65.

69. Ibid.

70. Russell Warren Howe and Sarah Hays Trott, *The Power Peddlers* (New York: Doubleday, 1977), p. 444.

71. Quoted in Mathias, p. 989.

72. Ibid.

73. Ibid.

74. Ibid., p. 997.

75. Ibid.

76. Joseph Dorision, "Jewish Politics: The Art of Survival," in Roucek and Eisenberg, eds., pp. 233–5.

77. Ibid., p. 237.

78. Gerson, p. 87.

79. Ibid., pp. 84–85.

80. Ibid., p. 90.

81. Frank E. Manuel, *The Realities of American-Palestine Relations* (Washington, D.C.: Public Affairs Press, 1949), pp. 176–8.

82. Gerson, p. 94.

83. Quoted in Stephen D. Isaacs, *Jew and American Politics* (New York: Doubleday, 1974), p. 243.

84. Ibid., p. 244.

85. Harry S. Truman, *Memoirs* (New York: Doubleday, 1956), 2:160.

86. Ibid., pp. 143–55.

87. Isaacs, pp. 244–5.

88. Ibid., p. 258.

89. Robert H. Trice, "Domestic Interest Groups and a Behavioral Analysis: The Arab-Israeli Conflict," in Said, ed., p. 121.

90. Mathias, p. 996.

91. Howe and Trott, p. 318. But despite Kissinger's opinion, the American Jewish community has not given up attempting to rescue Soviet Jews. Moreover, they continue to use the media to do so. Thus, when on January 2, 1985, the Union of Councils for Soviet Jews (UCSJ) placed a full page advertisement in the *Wall Street Journal* addressed to Secretary of State Schultz on behalf of seventy-three Soviet Jews, they appealed to him as a person of Jewish descent to plead their case when he met Soviet officials in Geneva the following week. The UCSJ had no doubt that ethnicity was an important factor in the foreign relations of the United States. The ad read (in part):

> We are appealing to you not to be indifferent to our predicament. Had your grandparents not emigrated from Russia, you too might be sharing our fate.... Remember—we share a common destiny.... Remember now, before the moment comes when hundreds of thousands of your brothers and sisters are sentenced to vanish. Forty years ago you were silent. Today you must speak for us and about us. Speak because our mouths are silenced.

There is no indication that the American secretary of state mentioned the plight of Soviet Jews when he spoke to the Soviets about the tensions between the United States and the USSR, especially that of arms control. But the UCSJ sponsors of the ad felt that it was important to remind the secretary of state of his ancestral links to certain Soviet citizens if only because they felt that, symbolic or not, ethnicity was an important factor in the relations between sovereign states.

92. Mathias, p. 996.

93. Carl W. Fell, "How 'Star Wars', Trade and Jewish Emigration Intertwine," *The Christian Science Monitor,* Jan. 29, 1985, p. 3.

94. Bailey, p. 30.

95. Ibid.

96. Ibid.

97. John H. Smyth to Frelinghuysen, October 2, 1882; Cited in Adelaide Cromwell Hill and Martin Kilson, eds., *Apropos of Africa* (London: Frank Cass and Co., 1969), pp. 94–97.

98. Ibid.

99. Smyth to Secretary of State, No. 69, Feb. 12, 1880; *Despatches from Liberia* (Washington, D.C.: National Archives), pp. 701-2.

100. Despatches of Apr. 7, 1880, from Secretary of State Evarts to E. F. Noyes, American minister to France. From MSS Records of State Department, Moore *International Law Digest,* 5 (1884), 767.

101. George Washington Williams, "An Open Letter to His Serene Majesty Leopold II, King of the Belgians and Sovereign of the Independent State of Congo, by Colonel the Honorable George W. Williams," cited in Hill & Kilson, p. 106.

102. Emmett J. Scott, "The American Commissioners in Liberia," *The Southern Workman,* 38 (1909), 556.

103. Rayford W. Logan, "The Historical Aspects of Pan-Africanism: A Personal Chronicle," *African Forum,* 1 (1965), 90ff.

104. Roi Ottley, *New World A-Coming* (Boston: Houghton Mifflin, 1943), p. 109.

105. W. E. B. DuBois, "The Inter Racial Implications of the Ethiopian Crisis," *Foreign Affairs,* 14 (1935), 88, 92.

106. W. E. B. DuBois, *The World and Africa* (New York: International Publishers, 1971), p. 255.

107. Elliott P. Skinner, "African, Afro-American, White American: A Case of Pride and Prejudice," *Freedomways,* 5 (1965), 384.

108. Elliott P. Skinner, "Afro-Americans and Africa: The Continuing Dialectic," pamphlet by The Urban Center, Columbia University (New York, 1973), pp. 16–17.

109. Rupert Emerson, "American Interests in Africa," *The Centennial Review,* 4 (1960), 416. See also Melville J. Herskovits, "Study of United States Foreign Policy in Africa," prepared for the Committee on Foreign Relations of the United States Senate, 86th Congress, 1st Session, Oct. 23, 1959, p. 14; W. Averell Harriman, quoted in *New York Times,* Oct. 9, 1960, p. 117; U.S. Congress, Senate Committee on Foreign Relations Study Mission to Africa, Nov.–Dec., 1960, 87th Congress, 1st Session, Feb. 12, 1961, p. 3.

110. Skinner, "African, Afro-American, White American," pp. 22–23.

111. Ibid.

112. "Resolutions," American Negro Leadership Conference on Africa (New York: Arden House, 1962).

113. *New York Times*, Dec. 12, 1970. Cited in Herschelle S. Challenor, "The Afro-American Connection," Phelps Stokes Seminars on Afro-American Relations, Oct. 1973, p. 47.

114. "U.S. Widens Ties to African Whites," *New York Times*, Apr. 2, 1973.

115. Charles C. Diggs, "Why We Should Not Be Involved in Angola," *New York Amsterdam News*, Jan. 10, 1976. Cf. Henry A. Kissinger, Department of State Bulletin, Mar. 1976.

116. "Caucus Urges Kissinger to Stimulate Positive African Relations," *New York Amsterdam News*, Apr. 24, 1976.

117. "The African-American Manifesto on Southern Africa," Sept. 25, 1976 (Washington, D.C.).

118. "Jimmy Carter on Africa," *Africa Report*, May-June 1976.

119. Henry F. Jackson, *From Congo to Soweto: U.S. Foreign Policy Toward Africa Since* 1960 (New York: William Morrow & Co., 1982), p. 77n.

120. "Statement on U.S. Relations with Africa," Washington, D.C., May 12, 1978, p. 3.

121. Chester A. Crocker, "Scope Paper: Your [i.e., Haig] Meeting with South African Minister Botha, May 14," *New York Times*, May 29, 1981.

122. Ibid.

123. Richard Leonard, *South Africa At War* (Westport, Conn.: Lawrence Hill & Co., 1983). See especially Appendix C, "The Crocker Documents on South Africa."

124. Study Commission on U.S. Policy Toward South Africa, *South Africa: Time Running Out* (Berkeley, Cal.: University of California Press, 1981), p. xvii.

CHAPTER VI

The American Character and the Formation of United States Foreign Policy

Introduction

*The authors of this chapter have had significant personal responsibility
and involvement in contemporary foreign affairs. Here they reflect on
their experience and what it has shown them about the American character, its motivation, and its limits upon foreign policy formulations.
McGeorge Bundy makes the provocative point regarding foreign policy
goals that "one cannot win them all." This wisdom is not easy for energetic
Americans, accustomed to solving problems, to accept.*

*McGeorge Bundy also shares his thoughts on the terrible power of nu-
clear weapons and his experience in the Cuban missile crisis. Does the ad-
vent of hydrogen bombs demand a radical rethinking of all our assumptions about our world, and whether war can be an instrument of policy? If
the security of the United States and the Soviet Union are, in effect, in each
other's hands, what does this imply about the methods of both implement-
ing policy and maintaining peace? What is "enough" in terms of nuclear
arms when only a hundred bombs dropped on either country could virtually destroy it?*

*Alton Frye, whose primary career has been at the Council on Foreign
Relations, has come to know many senior foreign policy professionals in
recent years, and his personal influence in this field is considerable. He believes that in spite of America's diverse cultural background and political
leanings, there is a strong element of national unity which surfaces in*

times of international crises. We may have had bitter disputes about the Vietnam War, for instance, but it was clearly a family argument. Mr. Frye points out that in spite of the vigor of American intentions in recent wars—Korea and Vietnam—it was finally a sense of moderation shared by Americans which kept the fighting within geographic and technological limits. Does this sense of moderation still exist, and will it enable us to work our way through nuclear issues?

McGEORGE BUNDY *was educated at Yale and Harvard Universities and served in the United States Army during World War II, seeing action in Sicily and taking part in the invasion of France. After the war, he was a consultant to the Economic Cooperation Administration in its administration of the Marshall Plan. He then returned to Harvard, was appointed professor of government, and in 1953 he became dean of the faculty of the arts and sciences. He served as special assistant to the president for national security affairs during the Kennedy and Johnson administrations. In 1966 he became president of the Ford Foundation from which he retired in 1979. He is now professor of history at New York University.*

ALTON FRYE *graduated from St. Louis University and received his Ph.D. from Yale in 1961. Since 1972, he has served at the Council on Foreign Relations, Inc., and since 1977 has been the council's Washington director and senior fellow. From 1968 to 1971 he was legislative and administrative assistant to Senator Brooke. He has also been a visiting professor at the University of California at Los Angeles, and he lectures often at institutions ranging from the University of Southern California to the National War College. Dr. Frye is consulted widely on matters of national security and has been a frequent contributor to newspapers and journals in the field of foreign policy and the military aspects of arms control.*

VI A
McGEORGE BUNDY

When you are trying to connect anything as large, complex, and varied as the American character to something as ever-changing, subtle, and increasingly multifarious in its operative forces as the international world, you are undertaking a task which is self-evidently beyond any one analyst, and still further beyond any one person in any one essay. All we can hope to do here is to offer a series of partial observations on aspects of this enormous subject.

In connecting Americans to foreign policy—as a country, as a people, as a whole—we have to start with the proposition that for most Americans foreign policy doesn't really matter, except when it does. That is to say, we do instinctively grow up and live in the belief that in this country society exists for its members, and not, on any sustained or continuous basis, the other way around. Obviously that is not always so, as we know from extraordinary moments of effort in times of national and international crisis. No country has shown—paradoxically in a civil war—a more intense dedication of individuals to the common good, or what was perceived as the common good, than our own. Older Americans still remember as a direct experience the enormous national effort that was produced by a fully shared sense of crisis and common cause in World War II.

We should also recognize, I think, in the forty postwar years, a remarkably steady and persistent national awareness that the United States is in fact needed as a necessary part of any peaceful international arrangement of power and politics. I hesitate to speak of a *balance* of power, important as that is, because I think the concept of a balance of power is not, in fact, one which commends itself strongly to the American mind. Until 1940 neither our history nor our politics included any experience or expectation that our own national destiny required both the acceptance and the management of international commitments based on the need to counter or contain or balance the power and ambition of others. What we thought we had done in World War I was either to punish the Hun for his unrestricted submarine warfare or to take part in a crusade to make the world safe for democracy. We had certainly not engaged ourselves to maintain an international balance of power, and the experience did not produce in most of us such new ways of thought.

However, it became apparent in the aftermath of World War II that we could not expect the Grand Alliance to continue in the fashion for which there had been such lively hope up through the time of Yalta and the founding of the United Nations. It became clear that there was indeed in the Soviet power a serious threat (unless it were countered, checked, or contained), a threat not only to nations indispensable to us as friends and partners, but even to ourselves. Ever since then we have been ready, with varying degrees of concern, alertness, and fear, to play a much larger and wider part. It is hardly to be wondered at that we have made mistakes and indulged in excesses; and we have sometimes found ourselves frustrated. In our own reactions to the changing decades we have had changing tempers among parts, and sometimes very large parts, of our own society.

On the whole, I think, the judgment that should fairly be rendered on the total performance of the United States since 1945 is not negative, but we have had painful lessons along the way. The hardest of them should, in one sense, have been easy for men and women of American character, because the most difficult thing we have had to find out is something that is epitomized in a remark we regularly make to one another after one of life's most frequent experiences—whether in sport or in business or in a classroom or elsewhere—the experience of losing. What we tell each other is, "You can't win 'em all." The fact that this commonplace and almost self-evident phenomenon also occurs in international conflict has come home to us with great pain and with a lack of national acceptance which we have with us still in the aftermath of Vietnam. The painful lesson that you cannot win them all, and the further lesson that if you do get into a loser you should be ready to cut your losses, are lessons we have been slow to learn and reluctant to accept.

There is some connection here with the element in the American view of the world which D. W. Brogan described in 1952 in an essay entitled "The Illusion of American Omnipotence."[1] Brogan did not mean that Americans in reality thought themselves all-powerful, but rather that they did think themselves somehow entitled to a certain immunity from international trouble, so that any situation which distressed or endangered the United States could exist "only because some elected or nonelected Americans are fools or knaves."[2] It is true that we are quick to blame one another when things go wrong, and one element in the polarization of our opinions over the last twenty years is surely the shared conviction of groups otherwise deeply opposed to one another that if it were not for bad *Americans,* leftist agitators for some and rampant militarists for others, things would be all right.

Brogan himself held that "belief in American invincibility is, on the whole, a good thing";[3] he compared it with the corresponding British belief in 1940, which "probably changed the history of the world." But it is one thing to be defiant in one's own defense and quite another to believe that such defiance can in itself determine the future of other societies than one's own. It may be that what we most need to do for ourselves in coming to terms with Vietnam is to understand that, whatever military mistakes we may have made, the record of American courage and battlefield success was in no decisive way unworthy of our past, and that our real mistake was in our refusal, for much too long, to recognize that the heavy and enduring imbalance between the Communist and anti-communist contenders in Vietnam, in military skill, political effectiveness, readiness for sacrifice, and internal unity, was not open to reversal by any level or length of American engagement short of nuclear war. A tradition of invincibility is helpful only when it is not stretched too far. British determination in 1940 did indeed change history, but one result of that victory was the "loss" of the empire, and it took British moderation to let India go in peace, accepting as inescapable the bloody partition that no British army could have stopped.

A different lesson we have, I think, learned rather better, although again not without pain, and that is the lesson that there are not many conflicts, perhaps not any, that you can expect to win completely. Especially in our competition with the Soviet Union, which is real and strong, we do not have it in our power, and because we are in the nuclear age it is not in our interest, to press the contest to an ultimate decision which we could try to win in the way we won the Second World War together. Neither of us can expect to win in that way. Indeed, in nuclear matters, if it ever comes to what is called in sterile and unreasonable language "an exchange," no one can win at all. I shall have more to say about that.

Somewhere between the unwinnability of a nuclear war and the inevitability of an occasional reverse, there is a third and more subtle lesson, that of the value of moderation, and I find two instances particularly interesting. The most obvious, I think, is the requirement of moderation in the necessary leadership of the United States in its relations with those who are formally or informally its allies. We have discovered repeatedly, and we have come on the whole to understand, that in an alliance of unequal democratic powers there is not in reality the kind of ready deference to the most powerful that many among us, in a first reaction, would expect to find. On balance, most conspicuously in the Atlantic alliance, we have been able to tolerate this troubling condition, recognizing, for example, that there can be a firm insistence among Belgians on deciding for themselves, in their own way, whether to accept a deployment of nuclear weapons which in overall terms is quite small. Years ago, in the case of France, our acceptance of the French right to act differently—to be *in* the alliance and *out* of the organization—proved essential to the survival of the whole undertaking. It has been so in other ways in other years with other allies.

Our greatest success in the resolution of grave danger by both strength and moderation came in the Cuban missile crisis. Here a president who insisted on what he believed his countrymen would require—the removal of Soviet nuclear missiles in Cuba—also insisted that it would be wrong, dangerous, and unproductive to insist on anything more. That restraint, which allowed the survival of the Castro regime, was sharply criticized in the years that immediately followed. It was not until much later that the president's use of a naval blockade came under substantial criticism from revisionists as too strong—not until a time when critics no longer remembered that what ultimately required the removal of the Soviet missiles was not the balance of strategic power but the intense conviction of the American people as a whole that those missiles simply did not belong in Cuba.

There is a problem here which we still find hard in our relations with countries that we perceive as our near neighbors. In the terms that are appropriate to nuclear delivery systems, the distance from the United States to Nicaragua, or to Cuba, is not much less than the distance from Soviet missile fields to Omaha, and certainly not less than the distance from Soviet submarines to Washington. But in psychological terms matters are different. We feel that the territory of the Western hemisphere is somehow "our" part of the world. We had the gravest difficulty in developing national public acceptance of the fair bargain over the Panama Canal which was at once a major achievement of the Carter administration and a severe charge upon that president's bank of political credit. Today in Central America we have not fully learned the lessons of moderation, although operationally we have respected the limits of our real interest more than our rhetoric has suggested.

In some measure, indeed, the Reagan administration has chosen to substitute posture for policy, especially in its dealings with Nicaragua. An economic embargo without international support, as no one has explained with greater force than George Shultz in other contexts, is notoriously ineffective, and attempts at military counterrevolution sponsored by the CIA have had an equally dismal record of failure. Yet rhetorically the stakes seem to go up as the months go by—these feeble and even counterproductive measures are defended on the ground that otherwise there will be one hundred million Communist slaves to our south, and tens of millions of refugees at our borders. Meanwhile a deaf ear is turned to the prudent, moderate, self-confident, and wholly non-Communist counsels of our best friends in the region. There is evidently unfinished business in our national way of thinking about nearby revolution when a government that has learned to live in friendship with a billion Red Chinese can find no way but covert war to coexist with three million Nicaraguans.

The most serious problem of all, simply because a failure to deal with it wisely would be so destructive, is the nuclear danger. The problem here is intensified for our citizenry as a whole by the degree to which it has been believed among us from the beginning (less now than then, but to a high degree all through) that somehow this problem belonged not to all of us, but really to the president. Everything about it seemed to contribute to that conclusion: its secrets, its extraordinarily complex physics and technology, its inescapable relationship to the behavior of the Soviet Union, a nation now as powerful as our own in the field, if not perhaps by some measures more so, and secretive in its nature, totalitarian in its management, inherently deceptive because of its conviction that truth is not safe in the hands of the imperialists. For all these reasons the nuclear problem has seemed to be one first for experts, and then in a different and larger sense one for the president. From the beginning of the nuclear age we have found ourselves thinking about what *the president* will recommend, and hoping that *the president* will give a lead. Harry Truman inherited both a terrifying secret and a habit of secrecy. Truman secretly decided that the weapon would help to win and that it should be used, and it was used. After that, while some of the secrets *about* the bomb might persist, the secret of its existence could not. Hiroshima was a most dramatic announcement to all the world of what was now a possibility. But people waited for the president's proposals. That has been more true than not ever since.

Yet what is interesting about the last ten or fifteen years is that we have begun to encounter criticism and debate on presidential decisions and recommendations which up to 1969 were always accepted, although sometimes affected in advance by pressure from the Congress. Throughout the Kennedy administration the problem of the deployment of new nuclear systems was bounded at the lower level by what the analysts thought would be enough, and at the upper level by what political leaders believed the Congress would require. Usually recommendations were near the upper end. In domestic political terms the hardest contest of the first year came from the president's decision to kill the B-70 bomber, a decision which did not have wide public support and required careful and sensitive bargaining with the powers on the Hill.

In 1969 all that began to change, and Americans found themselves for the first time in a national debate about a proposed new system, the antiballistic missile system of that time. The debate was not conspicuous for the dispassionateness of analysis. Feelings were high. Differences were acute. The question was resolved when the president of the day, Mr. Nixon, made his decision—a quite personal decision—that trading out the ABM was a better answer than fighting to build the system. The country applauded, and the resulting SALT I treaty was approved by a much wider margin than the limited test ban treaty which was the proudest achievement of the Kennedy administration, small as it was.

The underlying relation between American character, American expectations, American feelings, and nuclear danger remains unresolved. There have been moments of relative peace of mind. There was relative calm in the briefer-than-expected period of American monopoly; any country may be forgiven for believing that the world is safer if that country is the only one with the atomic bomb.

However, that experience was not altogether healthy, because it left us with a kind of instinctive belief that it was essential somehow, if we could not have a monopoly, at least to have an effective superiority. There followed after 1950 a period of fifteen to twenty years in which it was incumbent upon American presidents to assert and to maintain that they would attend to the maintenance of American superiority. There developed in the later years of Eisenhower and in the years of Kennedy and Johnson a serious difference between what presidents believed in their own minds and what they allowed and indeed encouraged the American people to continue to believe. Dwight Eisenhower understood with the same rapidity and clarity as Winston Churchill that the world had changed from the moment at which it became inevitable that two great powers (and others in turn, in all probability) would have survivable thermonuclear forces, the use of which by either one against the other would predictably receive a devastating reply. It was Churchill who said in one of his last great speeches that this was what the thermonuclear weapon would do, that this prospect was one which could not be avoided and should not be evaded, that it should be looked in the eye and that when you looked it in the eye you could find a prospect of hope. That hope lay in the anticipation of a time when "safety will be the sturdy child of terror and survival the twin brother of annihilation." The notion that there might be stability in a prospect of mutual assured destruction is not a theory developed by a later American administration. It is a condition of life in the thermonuclear age, and it was first described, with unparalleled eloquence and clarity, by a statesman in a third nation. I have always believed that the British perception of the reality of nuclear danger, which has been strong and clear from the very beginning, was enormously assisted by the fact that the difference that a nuclear weapon makes to the security of the British Isles is so obvious, so enormous, so inescapable. A nation which had been spared for nearly a millennium from invasion was exposed to a shock of recognition.

Given his whole record, it is not surprising that it was Winston Churchill who gave it the most eloquent expression.

We for our part are still in some degree a people trying to escape the vulnerability created by thermonuclear reality. You find that effort to escape as much among those who look for a time when these weapons can somehow be abandoned as you do among those who believe that safety is to be found only in the most remorseless accumulation of still greater stockpiles. You find it among ardent advocates of unilateral disarmament. You find it conspicuously in President Reagan's obvious and sincere hope that there is a defensive technical solution which can make the weapons "obsolete." I believe that sober second thought throughout this period has demonstrated over and over again that as long as you have the enormous adversarial sovereignties that you have in the United States and the Soviet Union, as long as thermonuclear weapons in small numbers continue to have a capacity for quick catastrophic devastation, as long as each side continues to have large survivable second-strike forces, and as long as the interaction of offensive and defensive technology is such that no honest man can ever look forward with any confidence to a leakproof defense, just so long we shall find ourselves living with the necessity of respecting nuclear danger and avoiding nuclear war.

No president at any time has fully educated the American people to these realities, so the American people have quite naturally divided among themselves and followed first one hope and then another. The wonder, in this subject as in foreign policy as a whole, is that we have not more dangerously lost our way. Yet what we have today in nuclear matters is a kind of polarization that is not altogether hopeful. There has been polarization on other issues of course—on Vietnam, on Central America, in earlier years over Korea, even on the question of joining the Atlantic alliance. We should not suppose that this kind of difference among us is foreign to our character, not at all. But I do myself believe that there remains a requirement, both in foreign policy as a whole and in this most conspicuous case of nuclear danger, for a more sustained and stronger effort than we have seen over the last decade to search out ground that can be common, if not to all of us, at least to most.

Let me try very briefly to say what I think the shape of that common ground may be in the field of nuclear danger. Its first element, I think, must be a shared recognition of the uniqueness of these weapons as compared to any others in history. Mr. Reagan has hold of one absolutely fundamental part of the truth when he tells us repeatedly that "A nuclear war cannot be won and must never be fought." But he does not tell us so clearly, and in fairness other presidents have not either, that when you make that statement you are also making the statement that we are required to maintain a peaceful coexistence with the government of the Soviet Union.

The psychological difficulties in accepting that second proposition are clear and strong. The reasons why we should wish and hope for a retreat of Soviet power, for instance from Eastern Europe, are evident. But the Soviet Union has its vital interests as we have ours, and the very fact that we must not have a nuclear war with the Soviet Union means that we cannot force a confrontation with much risk of war of any kind. We cannot press against what the Soviets see as their vital interests in a way that might strike the catastrophic spark, just as they for their part must show a similar restraint toward us. And in fact both sides do show such restraint. While we have had grave crises with the Soviet Union, not only in Cuba but also earlier in Berlin, what has been most striking about Soviet behavior in such moments of danger is its prudence, its caution, its resistance to running risks that might get out of control. I think the historical record shows, on both sides, a tendency to recognize the need for restraint in our actions, but not yet sufficiently in our words. Unfortunately, a lack of restraint in words or in what is called declaratory policy can be a fertile source of fear to others.

The next truth which I think we should be able to learn now about nuclear danger runs against our intuitions. The president gave us a remarkable example of the wrong way to think about it when in early 1985 he turned to the fourteenth chapter of Luke for an explanation of the need for strengthening our forces. In that chapter Jesus asked, "What king, going to encounter another king in war, will not sit down first and take counsel whether he is able with ten thousand to meet him who comes against him with twenty thousand? And if not, while the other is yet a great way off, he sends an embassy and asks terms of peace." The president then drew the moral in language that is pertinent to our theme: "I don't think the Lord who blessed this country, as no other country has ever been blessed, intends for us to have to some day negotiate because of our weakness."[4]

While Mr. Reagan did not apply the analogy drawn by Jesus to the specific case of nuclear weapons, he was in fact putting in biblical terms the precise argument that has been made over the last decade by the Committee on the Present Danger, a group which he has ardently supported and which in turn has supported him and placed many of its senior members in high positions in his administration. What that committee believes is precisely that an asserted Soviet superiority in heavy nuclear weapons will force us to accept Soviet coercion—in effect to negotiate from weakness. But while it is generally true that in the ordinary case twenty thousand men will beat ten thousand, it is not true at all that there is any decisive difference between ten thousand nuclear weapons and twenty thousand, as long as any significant fraction on either side will survive for use in retaliation.

In nuclear matters what President Eisenhower once called "the numbers game" is a most fertile source of error. Enough is enough. That is what Churchill meant, what Eisenhower understood, what Kennedy felt in his bones, but what only the Englishman took the time to explain clearly to his countrymen. It is time for us to get it clear in our heads that an unbreakable equality begins far below the levels now reached on both sides, that there is no leakproof escape in any kind of defensive system, that enough is indeed enough, and that the country which shows unilateral moderation is the country that is taking the political lead. I do not believe that this kind of understanding is beyond the American character, but I do think this kind of argument has yet to be presented by the people's leaders with the honesty and effectiveness that the people deserve.

These are examples from a rich and tangled history. They do not begin to exhaust the subject put before me. When one is asked to think of the achievement and performance of one's own country and to rate it, one should of course be disqualified as a passionately interested advocate, and not appointed or self-selected as a judge. But I do not think we need to work on the problems of the future with a governing sense that over the past we have failed. If we take the record of the United States in the world, the behavior of the American people in shaping that record since the fall of France when a change in the European balance did indeed produce an enormous requirement upon us for taking part; if we look at that record, and anyone says to us that it is unsatisfactory, we are entitled to imitate the man who was asked how he liked his wife and replied, "Compared to what?"

NOTES

1. Reprinted in *American Aspects* (New York: Harper & Row, 1964).
2. Ibid., p. 10.
3. Ibid., p. 11.
4. Remarks to the annual conference of the National Religious Broadcasters, Feb. 4, 1985; printed in *Weekly Compilation of Presidential Documents,* Feb. 11, 1985, p. 130.

VI B
ALTON FRYE

"When Shakespeare was alive, there were no Americans, . . . when Virgil was alive there were no Englishmen, . . . when Homer was alive, there were no Romans." Walter Lippmann's striking reminder is a useful starting point for any exploration of nationalism.

To discuss a nation's character is to enter a realm of metaphor and hyperbole, a region of fragmentary insight and large speculation. Perhaps that is why it has proved an irresistible topic for scholars of many nations and many philosophical hues. Since the early years of our republic, "the American character" has been a particularly fond subject for native and foreign observers, often observers of great distinction. And Americans have been fortunate to have perceptive critics to depict their qualities as a nation. On the whole, those scholars have treated us sympathetically, hailing the promise of our virtues and alerting us to the dangers of our vices. Yet the glimpses they have provided are merely that—reflections of a complex subject bathed in shadow.

In thinking about the American character and its influence on our conduct in the wider world, we can recognize ourselves in many famous interpretations. Alexis de Tocqueville captured something real about Americans when he saw their hallmark as a melding of egalitarianism with the pursuit of common goals through the formation of myriad associations and organizations. Frederick Jackson Turner identified a crucial factor in our national character when he stressed the importance of the frontier experience. So did David Potter when he argued that Americans are what they are in part because they have been a "people of plenty"—pioneers, yes, but pioneers in a land of abundance. Samuel Flagg Bemis underscored the fact that our pioneers were able to conduct their democratic experiment across a continental domain generally free from foreign interference, secure in their splendid isolation behind the broad expanse of two oceans—and a well-disposed British fleet. Oscar Handlin noted another significant dimension in his portrayals of the melting pot, the miraculous transformations wrought by the waves of immigration that gave new meaning to the phrase *e pluribus unum*. And David Riesman struck a sober counterpoint when he depicted *The Lonely Crowd* as a characteristic aspect of modern America that could well threaten the community's historic cohesiveness.[1]

Obviously, no one of these or other studies is an adequate guide to the American character, though each captures a valid aspect of our nationhood. The lesson I would draw from them is an elementary one: there are many more salient features to the American character than we have identified, and the weight assigned to any one feature rises and falls with the passage of time. The character of any nation is a fluid continuity, a psychic stream of human generations bearing elements of past experience and acquiring new experience. It resists definition because its constancies mingle tantalizingly with changes visible and invisible. In trying to relate such an elusive reality to the concrete issues of foreign policy, one traverses dense and tangled terrain. The rule here is: beware of sweeping generalizations, but remember they may be the best you can get.

One notes that many elements in the classic interpretations of American character are no longer unique to the United States. Canadians and Australians are also immigrant people, as are the Argentinians and the Brazilians. They too have coped with the frontier experience on a grand scale. Likewise, the Russians have faced the challenge of a vast frontier, though Siberia is far more arduous and less inviting than the Northwest Territory or Oregon. In the last quarter of the twentieth century, Germans and others have outstripped Americans as a people of plenty, at least if one measures per capita income. And the psychological isolation of individuals in mass society jeopardizes the sense of community in many modern, affluent nations. So elements in the American compound are present elsewhere, albeit in different proportions and in different settings.

Moreover, in assessing the influence of national character on foreign policy, one finds as many questions as answers in those familiar interpretations. Does America's material abundance impel the United States to approach other nations in a share-the-wealth spirit or in a determination to protect its standing as the rich man in the valley of the poor? Does the frontier tradition tempt the nation to cast covetous eyes abroad or to rest content within its established territory? Do memories of secure isolation portend withdrawal from world affairs or a disproportionate lashing out at others for disturbing that isolation? The questions suggest that the grand theories of American nationalism offer clues to understanding our modern character, but they yield no conclusive guides.

Perhaps we can penetrate the thicket better if we look beyond the grand theories to more operational notions. Can we discern the American character more clearly by examining what the nation believes about itself and other nations? Are there *characteristic* patterns of behavior in American foreign policy and are there characteristic national values displayed in that policy? Here we benefit from the availability of extensive survey research into the attitudes and values of the United States and other countries.

Some of the most striking findings of public opinion research concern the behavior of Americans in periods of international crisis. In moments of acute crisis there occurs what one might call a *huddling* phenomenon. When a sense of threat to the nation arises, American attitudes shift rapidly and markedly to support for the incumbent president, whoever he is and apparently without regard to whether or not he may have contributed to the crisis. This phenomenon is well known to politicians; virtually every presidential election now brings speculation of some "October surprise," that is, some international crisis late in the campaign that may work to the benefit of the incumbent. The Berlin crisis of 1948 demonstrably worked to President Truman's advantage; his popular approval ratings soared from 36 percent to 69 percent in that year's surveys. Lesser but similar surges marked President Eisenhower's introduction of Marines into Lebanon, John Kennedy's management of the Cuban missile crisis, and Gerald Ford's response to the Mayaguez incident. More puzzling is the fact that President Kennedy reaped a similar bonus in public support from the Bay of Pigs invasion in 1961, even while he himself acknowledged his government's disastrous handling of the episode. And Jimmy Carter, stranded with 29 percent approval in the summer of 1979 soared to 61 percent that fall— after the Iranians seized the American hostages. To be sure, that approval eroded steadily over the next year, but the evidence suggests that it did so because Carter was seen as not sufficiently effective in asserting the national interest to retrieve the American captives.

The pronounced tendency to rally around the president in a crisis is one indicator of the continuing force of American nationalism. However doubtful or self-critical Americans may be about particular foreign policies, they are in no doubt whatsoever that they share a common fate as a people and that, when tested by dangers in the outer world, they must stand together. No international institution, no global values, no appeals to our common humanity demonstrate such power to mobilize American opinion. Americans today are surely more cosmopolitan than past generations, but they remain nationalists, viewing the world in "we-they" terms.

The vitality of American nationalism is, it seems to me, the single most potent factor in the current phase of the nation's foreign policy. The resurgent nationalism and assertive foreign policy of the 1980s are quite different from what most commentators foresaw in the aftermath of the historic traumas of Vietnam and Watergate, coming in the wake of President Kennedy's assassination. At precisely the time some observers were worrying over the "end of the American century," the collapse of American will, the return to isolationism, the actual trends in national attitudes were headed in exactly the opposite directions. Americans were demanding not withdrawal from the world at large, but more potent engagement to protect the country's high stakes abroad. If the Vietnam syndrome has induced a degree of caution and skepticism about the feasibility of American involvement in particular conflicts, it has bred a greater demand to prevail in those conflicts which prove unavoidable.

Surveys conducted for the Chicago Council on Foreign Relations are persuasive in this regard.[2] Where a decade ago only 33 percent of the respondents favored a more important role for the United States as a world leader, and 21 percent wanted a less important role, by 1978 55 percent wanted a larger international role, with only 14 percent preferring a smaller one. These numbers reflect a popular demand for more successful engagement in world affairs. They correlate well with other long-term trends in American opinion. For most of the last quarter century Americans have been confident that United States power was increasing, but in the 1970s a majority expressed the view that the nation's power was in decline. A majority also perceived that the Soviet Union's power was increasing and that the United States was becoming less respected by other nations. Events of the 1970s also brought a measurable rise in Americans' "dislike" of the Soviet Union, from 52 percent to 78 percent. By 1980, a majority of Americans were displacing their customary priorities and saying that foreign affairs and national defense were even more important problems than the economy. One cannot explain recent elections primarily in terms of these trends, but surely the revival of national pride and determination played an important part in Ronald Reagan's 1980 success and 1984 landslide.

Thus, the response to Vietnam and the associated disorders of the age was not escapism but a heightened assertiveness. Was this the product of a combination of fear that failure in Southeast Asia would bring dangers elsewhere and of the need for vindicating the nobility of the purposes we could not achieve in Vietnam? Or was it rather simply a prudent judgment that there was "no exit" from American responsibilities in the wider world? Perhaps it was all those things. Whatever the sources of this resurgent nationalism, it brings with it evident risks and opportunities for the country's leadership. A wholesome nationalism, creatively led, can energize American diplomacy, just as an absence of national self-confidence can sap the government's capacity to conduct foreign policy. But resurgent nationalism, less creatively led, can also feed pernicious policies and self-defeating initiatives. It can, for example, blind leaders to the legitimate interests of allies and provoke needless frictions over such issues as European gas pipeline deals with the Soviet Union or a bootless quest for an unachievable military superiority over the other superpower.

It is a familiar critique of nationalism in general, and Americanism in particular, that it tends to veer toward a secular religiosity that is incapable of compromise with others. Our nation's history is replete with such tendencies: "Give me liberty or give me death!"; "Fifty-four forty or fight!"; Wilson's "crusade for democracy"; Roosevelt's insistence on "total victory." Those instincts persist in the American psyche. Encounters with recalcitrant foreign states may cause them to erupt.

Yet those inclinations have been modulated in important ways. Truman's popularity plummeted during the Korean War, but he held the nation on a course of limited military action for limited aims that bespeaks a more measured United States approach to the world—and that looks wise in hindsight. The man he fired, Douglas MacArthur, asserted that "there is no substitute for victory"; but late in his life he came to terms with modern reality and concluded that, in nuclear war, there would be no distinction between victor and vanquished.

As one looks back at Lyndon Johnson's presidency, one recalls how anxious he was not to arouse a war fever in the country, lest policy become captive to popular passions for conclusive military success in Southeast Asia. Johnson's policy eventually failed, but its objectives were never cast in the absolute mold of earlier wars. Trying to apply what he thought were the lessons of Korea, Johnson introduced half-a-million United States troops not to destroy an enemy, but in the vain hope that deployment of such awesome force would intimidate the North Vietnamese.

I cite these points not to imply that Americans have outgrown their propensity to wage wars as crusades, but to note that there is some evidence of a capacity for more discriminating policy. More significantly, these episodes offer a degree of assurance that disappointments in pursuit of limited measures do not always prompt Americans to opt for more extreme measures. The painful truth is that the perceived failure of a relatively restrained policy may breed pressures to abandon the restraints rather than reconsider the goals. But whatever else may be said of American behavior in Korea and Vietnam, it did not lead automatically to the unlimited wars associated with indiscriminate nationalism. It is, I think, a sign of maturity in a powerful nation that frustration does not necessarily lead to escalation.

We need to recognize both the promise and the peril of post-Vietnam nationalism. On balance, I believe it is a welcome development because, in a world of nation-states, the prospects for a humane and constructive international order continue to depend on vigorous American participation. To overstate the point but slightly, American nationalism is an indispensable, if insufficient, condition for successful internationalism in our time. I hold the customary American view that it will be better for the United States—and better for the world—if we play an active part in international affairs. But whether that judgment is sound depends entirely on how we play that part.

If the ordeal of Vietnam triggered a revived nationalism, it also drew forth other complex responses from Americans. Many have lamented the debilitating self-criticism evoked in the United States, the divisions and alleged lack of public stamina that made it impossible for the country to persist in a costly conflict of uncertain duration and unpredictable outcome. Yet one may see in the protracted anguish of that period more positive qualities, particularly a capacity for self-correction when the ratio of necessary violence to expected achievement grew disproportionate.

The brutal summary of one former policy maker is apt. "What we really learned in Vietnam," he said, "is that the North Vietnamese and Vietcong were more willing to die for it than we were willing to kill for it." We learned that lesson too slowly, but it is not a bad quality for a nation to insist that ends and means be kept in balance, particularly when the means involve the use of force in circumstances where the enemy and the innocent are so difficult to distinguish. One may see in the public pressures for disengagement from Vietnam a wholesome adaptability that conditions the strong nationalistic currents. That adaptability is a saving grace, promoting a mature nationalism when intransigent pursuit of the nation's goals would be a recipe for perpetual conflict.

Recent movements in American opinion reveal some other notable characteristics—a capacity to sustain old friendships and to form new ones. Overwhelming majorities have clung to our NATO commitments as ones worth keeping. Although two-thirds of Americans feel they are carrying too much of the burden of defending the West, they are quite decisive in the verdict that United States troops should be used to thwart any Soviet invasion of Western Europe. Sympathy for Israel remains a strong component of American opinion. But consider other findings of recent vintage. In the wake of normalization of relations with the Peoples' Republic of China, the American people seem to have cut the psychological ties that bound them for so long to defending the Nationalist regime on Taiwan; only 18 percent would favor using American troops if China invaded Taiwan, fewer than the percentage who would be prepared to send troops to China if the Soviets were to invade. Most Americans disapproved of the dispatch of United States forces to Lebanon, just as they oppose their use in Central America, even though El Salvador is considered more important than Vietnam was.

De Tocqueville saw rigidities in American attitudes, pointing to the "difficulty of shaking the majority in an opinion once conceived of."[3] Nevertheless the last decade has shown extraordinary flexibility in popular attitudes toward a number of countries, several of which weigh crucially in the calculus of United States foreign policy. In 1976, only a third of Americans considered Egypt, Saudi Arabia, and Jordan as "friendly" countries. Spurred by Anwar Sadat's bold initiatives, by 1982 that number leaped to 78 percent who counted Egypt a friend, and majorities who felt that way toward the Saudis and Jordanians. Evidently, these shifts create an altered political context for diplomacy in the Middle East. They also suggest the mutability of American attitudes in an age of global communications. While the rapidity of such changes can work for or against sensible diplomacy, they may at least diminish the problem often cited by critics of the public's impact on foreign policy, namely the tendency for diplomatic requirements and popular attitudes to be seriously out of phase.

There are perplexities and contradictions in the structure of American opinion on foreign affairs. Its pluralistic roots give it a remarkable blend of sturdy patriotism and sense of connectedness to other lands and peoples. Much has been said, and deservedly so, of the ethnic politics which bear upon United States foreign policy. Americans of Greek extraction have felt a special concern about the Turkish invasion of Cyprus, and it has affected the nation's policy toward that region. Those of Eastern European descent, particularly from Poland, have been an obvious factor in the movements of our policy toward Soviet satellites, inviting the "captive nations" rhetoric and undergirding efforts aimed at reversing the outcome of the Yalta accords. For many decades those of Irish stock have provided sympathy and resources for revolutionary forces in Ireland.

Not all of these ethnic ties pose serious complications for United States foreign policy, but many of them contain that potential. Experience indicates, however, that assimilation and loyalty to the United States regularly prevail in any contest of fealty between the New World and the Old. Americans of German ancestry underwent the maximum tests in the First and Second World Wars, during both of which leaders in Berlin mistakenly counted on their emigrant countrymen to temper American policy toward Germany. In 1916, a German foreign ministry official declared that the United States would not enter the European war because there were five million Germans in the United States who would prevent intervention by force if necessary. The American ambassador replied grimly that, if there were five million Germans in the United States, there were five million and one lampposts. In the event, the two great wars drastically diminished the cultural links between

Americans and Germany, as German-language papers and other immigrant institutions virtually disappeared, names were changed, and new loyalties to the adopted land supervened.

In a basic sense, the choice for America in any direct conflict with an ancestral homeland is preordained. The very fact of immigration bespoke a judgment in favor of the United States, and for most citizens that judgment has been powerfully reinforced. Few Americans remain "hyphenated" for very long, and I believe we should not prolong the period by speaking of them as such. Yet most divergences between United States interests and those of foreign states do not reach the stage of overt conflict, and the sentiments of citizens may be more subtly balanced on issues short of war.

Here we touch on delicate matters. Politicians who speak openly of their concern about the distorting impact of ethnic groups on American policy find it arouses wide misunderstanding and frequent political reprisals by the groups in question. Such reactions are regrettable, although understandable if the main implication of references to ethnic politics is to cast doubt on a group's primary loyalties. But scholars are permitted, indeed obliged, to address reality without calculating likely voter reaction. Ethnic politics are bound to remain a major factor in United States policy toward a number of critical international issues. That is true, above all, for problems in the Middle East, Africa, and Latin America. Americans of Jewish, African, and Hispanic origins have special concerns about those regions and they are making their weight felt in related policy debates. The scale of United States military and economic assistance to Israel, the preoccupation with injustice in South Africa, the intense arguments over immigration reform—in these and other instances, ethnic groups do not dictate policy, but they do much to set the agenda and affect the outcomes.

If that were the whole reality, one might fear that our foreign policy could never gain coherence, that it could never be more than a mosaic of special interests. But ethnic groups are not merely claimants on American foreign policy; they may also contribute to its effectiveness. To take the most telling case, the Jewish community in the United States is a factor not only in American policy, but in Israeli policy. This country's ties to Israel consist of far more than the presence of many Jews in the United States; their presence also can be an important asset in United States relations with Israel. The Jewish community has been stalwart in its support for Israel, massively generous in its philanthropy, deeply respectful of those who created a new homeland for survivors of the holocaust. But those very ties give it standing in Israel—standing to press for pursuit of the Camp David process, to caution Israeli leaders when they appear impervious to world opinion, to convey credible demands for restraint if Israeli policy grows too militant. This is not to say that the Jewish community performs those functions consistently or self-consciously, but I believe it is true that Americans of Jewish descent have become a moderating and sensitizing force on an Israeli government forever prone to feel that it stands alone against a hostile world—and often disposed toward a Masada complex. The outrage among American Jews about recent events in Lebanon surely reinforced the second thoughts in Israel and helped to promote the gradual Israeli withdrawal.

In this domain, the preservation of domestic harmony and effective policy making require self-restraint on the part both of the pluralistic majority and of the ethnic minority. Ethnic groups are often caught in emotional cross-pressures that affect their political behavior; it behooves them to be aware that an excess of zeal or single-minded advocacy can invite the suspicion of other citizens. They carry an obligation to demonstrate through persuasion, not political coercion, that their recommendations serve the national interest. At the same time, other Americans have a responsibility to treat the claims of ethnic politics on their merits, not to dismiss them automatically as self-serving or contrary to the national interest. For it is only through a process of mutual accommodation and scrupulous decision making that the American community can forge a foreign policy sensitive to ethnic concerns, but governed by larger considerations.

Overhanging all discussion of contemporary foreign policy is the truly new circumstance of the United States in our time. One can describe that circumstance in a single word: vulnerability. Whether one speaks of the economic interdependence which binds American prosperity to that of other nations or of national security on a globe subject to nuclear catastrophe, citizens of the United States have, once and for all, lost their immunity to the perils of international politics. Most Americans know this, but it is not clear how they are adjusting to it. Americans' response to the unprecedented vulnerability which they now face may do more to shape and to test their national character than anything in history. So far the record is mixed, troubling but not hopeless.

A large percentage want to see progress on arms control; a similar number would be "willing to risk the destruction of the United States rather than be dominated by the Russians." The latter impulse may seem apocalyptic, but it relates to the social value most precious to Americans, the freedom for which they are still prepared to die. The finding is also an artifact of polls which pose the issue as "better Red than dead," when, as General Andrew Goodpaster has often remarked, most people would prefer to be "neither than either." Wrestling with their anxieties about nuclear weapons and their profound mistrust of the Soviet Union, Americans have favored both a robust defense program and earnest negotiations. Thus, the nuclear freeze movement was a form of demand-side politics, less a signal of national commitment to a specific negotiating program than of deep grass-roots desire for the government to move forward with hard-headed but good-faith efforts at arms control.

There is a healthy awareness among Americans regarding the overriding danger of nuclear war. Nine out of ten citizens believe that such a war would destroy both the United States and the Soviet Union, a much firmer view than existed three decades ago and one appropriate to the greatly enlarged nuclear arsenals in both countries. Most Americans think United States and Soviet nuclear capabilities are "about equal," and they seem to have drawn the logical conclusion that neither side could threaten to use such weapons with impunity. Mutual deterrence is well established in the minds of Americans; three-quarters of them oppose the use of nuclear weapons to meet a Soviet invasion of Western Europe, largely because they are convinced that escalation to all-out nuclear war would be inevitable. A preponderant majority feels that building more nuclear weapons would lead the Soviets to do the same thing, but that abolishing such weapons entirely is not a realistic possibility. Although American attitudes on these issues are not uniform, they display a surprising consistency in striving to balance deep mistrust of the Soviet Union with a rational quest for diplomatic regulation of the nuclear competition.

But the ambition for negotiated restraint on nuclear weapons struggles with a lingering hope that technology will rescue us from the plight of vulnerability. Few things are more typical of an inventive people than to look to technology for solutions when problems arise. It is not surprising that President Reagan is excited by the prospect that his strategic defense initiative will lift the terrible threat posed by offensive nuclear weapons. That initiative is a technological response to nuclear *angst*, just as the freeze campaign was a political response. Neither technology nor politics, by itself, is likely to prove sufficient. The profound question for Americans will be how to balance these technological and political impulses.

To strike a pragmatic balance, we shall need to be clear about the uniqueness of the technological condition in which we find ourselves. In speaking of the lofty possibilities of science, Einstein said that "God may be subtle, but he isn't mean."[4] He meant that man could pursue knowledge of the physical universe with confidence in its predictability and knowability; God would not change the rules of nature merely to frustrate the inquiring scientist. But the search for a technological escape from our nuclear plight is not a contest of man against nature; it is one of man against man. There is an adversary who is prepared to compete technologically to make sure that our vulnerability remains as great as his. For that reason, it is most unlikely that there can be a technological success in reducing our nuclear vulnerability unless there is a political success in defining which technological options are mutually agreeable to the United States and the Soviet Union.

It is not clear how well Americans and their leaders understand the premise that politics and technology must work together; otherwise one or the other will defeat efforts to relieve the growing vulnerability of both superpowers. There are some encouraging signs. Ronald Reagan began his second term with a markedly different stance from the one with which he entered office. A president who once seemed less sensitive than he should to the hazards of nuclear war now declares repeatedly that such a war can never be won and must never be fought. He has moderated his rhetoric and taken new diplomatic steps towards the Soviet Union, including his abandonment of the declared goal of military superiority. One detects in these developments not only the fruits of on-the-job training for a chief executive untutored in nuclear policy, but also a heightened sensitivity to public and congressional desire to repair the superpower relationship and to get on with intensive arms negotiations.

Although senior figures in the administration may still be divided on key questions of strategic policy, there are indications that the United States government recognizes that it could not move forward unilaterally with development and deployment of extensive defenses. After meeting with Foreign Minister Andrey Gromyko at Geneva, Secretary George Shultz emphasized that the current priority must be to seek substantial reductions in offensive forces and to end the erosion in the treaty limiting deployment of antiballistic missile defenses. If research on the so-called "star wars" program is confined to activities permitted by the ABM treaty—and Congress will have something to say about that—there will be time for thorough explorations with the Soviets to determine which political and technological arrangements we will both consider acceptable and conducive to stability.

One trusts that traditional American pragmatism will steer events in that direction. Because of its adaptability and innate pluralism, the robust nationalism of modern America remains capable of applying measured judgment to the hard choices demanded in foreign policy. None will be so demanding as those posed by the chronic vulnerability technology now imposes. When he came to the United States after the Civil War, Georges Clemenceau wrote that "there is fortunately a strange ability to bend with the wind, to recognize and profit from mistakes, to change courses, thanks to which pessimistic predictions are almost always quickly proven false."[5] Those qualities remain, and they offer hope that Americans will survive the dangerous passage that lies ahead.

NOTES

1. See David M. Potter, *People of Plenty: Economic Abundance and the American Character* (Chicago: University of Chicago Press, 1954); Samuel Flagg Bemis, *A Diplomatic History of the United States* (New York: Holt, 1950); Oscar Handlin, *The Uprooted: The Epic Story of the Great Migrations That Made the American People* (New York: Grosset and Dunlap, 1951); David Riesman, Nathan Glazer, and Reuel Denney, *The Lonely Crowd: A Study of the Changing American Character* (New Haven, Conn.: Yale University Press, 1950).

2. John F. Rielly, ed., *American Public Opinion and U.S. Foreign Policy 1983* (Chicago: The Chicago Council on Foreign Relations, 1983), pp. 11, 14, 19.

3. On Alexis de Tocqueville's view of the potential tyranny of majoritarianism in America, see Max Lerner, *America as a Civilization* (New York: Simon and Schuster, 1957), pp. 398, 671-2, 938-9. De Tocqueville is quoted and the data here are from surveys by Louis Harris published in *Public Opinion*, 5 (Apr.–May 1982), 53. For other data summarized here see the same periodical, 6 (Aug.–Sept. 1983), 25-26, 29.

4. Quoted in Norbert Wiener, *The Human Use of Human Beings: Cybernetics and Society* (Garden City, N.Y.: Doubleday, 1954), p. 35.

5. Quoted in Marc Pachter and Frances Stevenson Wein, eds., *Abroad in America: Visitors to the New Nation, 1776–1914* (Reading, Mass.: Addison-Wesley, 1976), p. 173.